Keighley, Past and Present: or, An Historical, Topographical and Statistical Sketch

William Keighley, Robert Holmes

Copyright © BiblioLife, LLC

BiblioLife Reproduction Series: Our goal at BiblioLife is to help readers, educators and researchers by bringing back in print hard-to-find original publications at a reasonable price and, at the same time, preserve the legacy of literary history. The following book represents an authentic reproduction of the text as printed by the original publisher and may contain prior copyright references. While we have attempted to accurately maintain the integrity of the original work(s), from time to time there are problems with the original book scan that may result in minor errors in the reproduction, including imperfections such as missing and blurred pages, poor pictures, markings and other reproduction issues beyond our control. Because this work is culturally important, we have made it available as a part of our commitment to protecting, preserving and promoting the world's literature.

All of our books are in the "public domain" and some are derived from Open Source projects dedicated to digitizing historic literature. We believe that when we undertake the difficult task of re-creating them as attractive, readable and affordable books, we further the mutual goal of sharing these works with a larger audience. A portion of BiblioLife profits go back to Open Source projects in the form of a donation to the groups that do this important work around the world. If you would like to make a donation to these worthy Open Source projects, or would just like to get more information about these important initiatives, please visit www.bibliolife.com/opensource.

64 Ancient family
74 Cavendish
129 Newsholme

ARMS OF THE KEIGHLEYS
OF KEIGHLEY AND INSKIP.

KEIGHLEY, PAST AND PRESENT;

OR,

AN HISTORICAL, TOPOGRAPHICAL,

AND

STATISTICAL SKETCH

OF THE

TOWN, PARISH, AND ENVIRONS

OF

KEIGHLEY,

INCLUDING

Riddlesden, Marley, Hainworth, and some other places in the contiguous

PARISH OF BINGLEY:

LIKEWISE

AN ACCOUNT OF THE ANCIENT FAMILIES WHICH HAVE FLOURISHED THEREIN, WITH A BRIEF MEMOIR OF THE REV. THEODORE DURY, M.A., LATE RECTOR OF KEIGHLEY.

LONDON:
ARTHUR HALL, VIRTUE & Co., 25, PATERNOSTER ROW.
KEIGHLEY : R. AKED; AND ALL BOOKSELLERS.
M DCCC LVIII.

PREFACE.

*"Of old, those met rewards who could excel,
And those were praised who but endeavoured well."*

We have often been amused with reading long prefaces to little books, wherein the writers have studiously anticipated objections and apologized for defects by the ostensible plea that their productions were never intended for publication. We shall, however, be silent on most of the objections which might be urged against many of our statements, and leave them for the critical reader to ponder over, hoping that his criticisms may be the means of eliciting some useful facts; and we have no apology to offer for appearing before the public, except a desire to extend and preserve the little we know of our native place and neighbourhood, by adding this humble contribution to our local literature.

The following pages contain the matured results of much diligent inquiry and research, continued for a series of years by the late Mr. William Keighley of Keighley. He laid every accessible source under tribute, and spared no labour to secure accuracy. Although the field of investigation is extensive, the materials which it affords are unusually scanty. Beyond a few incidental notices of Keighley in Domesday Survey, and documents chiefly relating to pedigrees, we have scarcely any historical data before the reign of Queen Elizabeth; even the parish register goes no farther back than the year 1562. One of the oldest and most interesting documents connected with the place is a manuscript narrative of events relating to the Quakers, from the year 1654 to 1760, and of which we have availed ourselves. We have recently been informed that Jennings's MSS. in the British Museum contain some notices of Keighley, but of what kind we are not aware.

As we have had to cull our information from a great variety of imperfect sources, it cannot be expected to be free from errors. Every person acquainted with subjects of this nature knows how difficult it is to obtain perfect accuracy. The correction of a single date or fact sometimes involves an incredible amount of labour. We have experienced this in attempting to reconcile the discrepancies in the pedigree of the family of Keighley, and clear up the uncertainty of the date of Gilbert Keighley's tombstone: our utmost endeavours have been unavailing, even with the assistance of our friend, Mr. Jonathan Hindle, whose intimate acquaintance with such subjects is well known. We have, in a few instances, supplied the want of certainty by probability, grounded upon reasons which are not always fully stated, as we did not wish to swell the book by what we deemed to be unnecessary details.

We would direct the reader's special attention to the invaluable meteorological observations under the head "Braithwaite;" we believe there are none collected in Yorkshire equal to them in length of time.

In drawing up the sketch of the life of our late worthy pastor, the Rev. Theodore Dury, the editor begs to tender his thanks to those friends who have supplied him with information; and he hopes that his own admiration of Mr. Dury's character has not caused him to speak too highly of his merits in the estimation of those persons who only knew him in a general way, as he is quite sure that those who knew him intimately will deem the memoir to be far below the deserts of the subject.

We had thought of adding some particulars respecting the natural history of the locality, but upon investigation we found neither animals, vegetables, nor minerals peculiar to the place; the subject is, therefore, only noticed incidentally.

Our remarks on those subjects which are ever fluctuating, such as trade, population, &c., are to be referred to their condition as they existed in the summer of 1857.

In order to preserve a clear and easy style throughout, we have taken the liberty of altering a few words in some of the quotations.

If any merit attaches to the historical portion of this unpretending volume, it may be offered as balm to perpetuate the memory of the late Mr. Keighley,— all literary defects must be ascribed to the editor,

ROBERT HOLMES.

Sunk Island, near Hull,
June, 1858.

CONTENTS.

	Page.
Situation of the Town	13
Pronunciation and Origin of its Name	16
Extract from the Domesday Survey	18
The Parish Church	21
The Rectory	36
St. John's Church	36
St. Mary's Church	38
King's Mill and Consolidated Manors	39
Market, Fairs, and Free Warren	42
Flodden Field	46
Military Occupation of the Town	48
Thoresby's Visit to this Town	50
Further Extracts from Mr. Gale's MSS.	51
The Free Grammar School	54
The Lower Free School	58
Court of Requests and County Court	59
Prevailing Customs and former Amusements	60
Ancient Custom of Tolling the Passing Bell	62
Ancient Family of Keighley	64
Noble Family of Cavendish	74

	Page.
Roman Roads and Coins	76
Celts, Urns, and other Antiquities	79
Dissenting Places of Worship.—Independents	82
Society of Friends	84
Wesleyan Methodists	92
Swedenborgians	94
Baptists	94
Methodists' New Connexion	95
Primitive Methodists	95
Keighley Mechanics' Institution	97
Halls and Villas	101
Armorial Bearings of the Neighbouring Gentry	103
Trade and Manufactures	105
Statistical Remarks	112
Increase of the Smiths	117
Keighley made a Polling Station	118
The Keighley Union	118
The Bursting of Crowhill Bog, with Annals of the Town's Further Progress	119
Villages and other Objects in the Neighbourhood	125
The Hitching Stone	127
Slitheryfore	129
Newsholme	129
Holm-house	131
Goose-eye	131
Laycock	132
Braithwaite, with Meteorological Observations	136
Fell Lane	139
Jennet's Well	140
The South-west or Sun-side of the Parish	141
Oakworth	145
Thwaites	151
Utley	155

	Page.
Holden Cliff and Park	158
Riddlesden Hall	160
West Riddlesden Hall	165
The Altar and Hamlet of Marley	168
Hainworth	174
Hermit-hole and Goff Well	178
The Rectors of Keighley.—Rev. Miles Gale	180
Memoir of the Rev. Theodore Dury	183

HISTORY OF KEIGHLEY.

SITUATION OF THE TOWN.

In former times, when the pack-horse was the principal medium for the conveyance of goods, and the fine easy roads and expeditious railways, which now, like network, cover the land, were unknown and unnecessary for the purposes of trade, the only access to the town of Keighley was by means of uneven paths which passed over the high and barren moors, by which it is surrounded. From the brows of those hills, the observant traveller, in past centuries, might look down with some degree of interest upon the rural place beneath, with its Manse and Manor-house, its Market-cross and Church on the green, skirted on the north and east with open pasture, bounded in the rear by thick woods and the meandering Aire, and on the south and west with lively streams and copse-covered knolls. Hence, we need not be surprised that some of the early writers have described it as being situated in a low valley, or the bottom of a deep glen; whilst, in fact, if viewed from the elevated ground on the north or north-west, it will be found to be placed at the south-western extremity of a pretty extensive alluvial plain, opening into the valley of the Aire—a very suitable site for a pastoral inland town, and well adapted to meet the simple wants of its early founders.

Before the extirpation of the extensive forests which seem to have abounded in Airedale, even crowning, in many instances, its lofty mural precipices, this portion of the fertile and umbrageous tract, relieved by open glades and green holmes, studded with farm houses and cottages, sheltered by high heathy ground of varied beauty, rich in lateral springs and rivulets flowing away to the gentle river as it glides in gentle curves along the plain, would present a sweet home scene on which a lover of nature might wish to linger. The hills, though high, do not attain to the character of mountains, unless Rumbles Moor be allowed that distinction, whose height is 1,322 feet above the level of the sea, and the elevation in the extreme west of the parish, which spurs off from Boulsworth, whose summit rises 1,697 feet.

That native woods and natural swamps have been transformed, by the persevering efforts of past generations, into luxuriant meadows and well-drained pastures, will appear evident on contrasting their present appearance with the names which they have for ages borne; such as the Flush, Sandywoods, Lawkholme, (in old deeds, Lake Holme) Eastwood, and Stubbings, most of which places being, until very recently, inundated with water during the winter season. It is no wonder, then, that when highways first became necessary, our forefathers, not caring to encounter the impervious wood and impassable morass, chose to construct them over the high hills, leaving their sapient and inquisitive posterity to indulge in idle speculation on the seeming absurdity. But if we consider the above facts, in connexion with the turbulent state of the country, when the unlettered barons ruled like petty kings in their respective territories, and often issued from their castles, with armed retainers, to commit depredations upon their weaker neighbours, or to settle a dispute with bow and sword, the apparent absurdity will resolve itself into a wise expediency.

In "Baines's History and Directory of the County of York," and the several works of the same kind which have appeared since its publication, the Parish of Keighley is represented as included in the Craven District, Wapontake of Staincliffe, and the liberty of Clifford's Fee; which statement, though correct in the main part, is not so in the whole; for a portion of it presents the singular anomaly of being situated in one division of the County, whilst it acknowledges the jurisdiction of another. "The Wapontake of Staincliffe excludes part of the parishes of Addingham and Keighley, and the whole of Bingley and Ilkley."* The line which divides the Skyrack division from East Staincliffe, commences where the water of South Cliffe enters the Sun Beck, cuts Lowstreet about the middle, divides the Township of Morton from Kildwick Parish, and proceeds northwards through Addingham. This boundary line was

---

* Introduction to the Second Edition of "Whitaker's History of Craven."

well known to the suitors of the District Court, previous to the introduction of the Court of Requests; and the ancient boundary-stone, in Low-street, was distinctly remembered by the aged of the last generation. The Parish averages about seven miles in length, by two and a quarter in breadth, and contains 10,160 acres and 14 hamlets: there is no dependent township. The names of the hamlets are, Braithwaite, Bogthorn, Dockroyd, Exleyhead, Fell lane, Harehill, Ingrow, Knowle, (or Knoll) Laycock, Newsholme, Oakworth, Slipperyford, Sykes, Utley, each of which will be noticed in the course of the narrative.

The latitude of the town, taking the parish church as the point, is 53° 51′ 55″ north, and 1° 54′ 28″ west longitude; and it is 366 feet above the sea level.

PRONUNCIATION AND ORIGIN OF ITS NAME.

Dr. Whitaker, the historian of Craven, who probably considered the tedious display of etymological lore as beneath his notice, informs us that "Kihel, or Kikel, is a Saxon proper name, and Keighley is the field of Kikel." But probably the details of a correspondence which lately took place in the *Manchester Guardian* on the pronunciation and supposed origin of the word, may not be inappropriately introduced in this place. The editor of that journal, in answer to the inquiry of 'A. S.' of Wakefield, whether the name of this place ought to be pronounced as 'Keathley' or 'Keely,' observes:—"The true pronunciation of the word is neither of those mentioned by our correspondent, but requires the guttural of the *gh*, which, except in the names of one or two places, has disappeared from the English language, though retained in the German and other kindred tongues. It is found in the ordinary pronunciation of 'Leigh,' (in Lancashire) and is occasionally heard in the pronunciation of Keighley; but the latter is more generally pronounced Keithley." To this reply the following was added by another correspondent:—

"Sir,—As a native of the town of Keighley, I felt much gratified by your answer to the inquiry of 'A. S.' of Wakefield, in the *Guardian* of June 7th, whether the name of that place ought to be pronounced as Keathley or Keeley; and believing that a few more words on the subject may not be unacceptable to some of your readers, beg leave to add, that notwithstanding the name of the place in former times was spelled in a variety of ways, yet the most common and genuine orthography appears to have been Kyghley—derived (as is supposed) from *kye* or *kine*, and *ley*, a field, meaning, in modern language, simply the cow-field, or cow-pasture; and till nearly the close of the last century was invariably spelled Kighley, the *e* having been obtruded, as it were, upon the inhabitants by their distant correspondents, since the town began to derive some degree of importance from its manufactures, in order, probably, to make the spelling agree more closely with the native pronunciation. The guttural sound of the *gh*, as you observe, is fast dying away, and the nearest approach to it, or to the present orthoepy of the word, will be Keethlah. Individuals at a distance generally pronounce its name either as Keelee, or Kiilee, which, to the native ear at least, sounds extremely finical and absurd."

As an illustration of the difficulty of pronouncing Keighley, and incidentally of its comparative obscurity, or, it may be, the ignorance of the questioner, a certain peer, a few years ago, in his place in parliament, having occasion to mention the name, exclaimed, "Keelee! where is Keelee?"

Though the history of a town like this, just emerging, as it were, from a state of obscurity, and unassociated in past times with the Monastery or the Castle, may present few incidents of a striking or important nature, yet surely in this christian, enlightened, and inquiring age, the writer needs not hesitate, or approach his subject with fear and trembling, merely because in days of yore no frowning castle stood, where

> "The yeoman tall
> The iron-studded gates unbarr'd,
> Rais'd the portcullis's pond'rous guard,
> The lofty palisade unsparr'd,
> And let the draw-bridge fall."

Taking local names as our guide to the early settlers in this part of Airedale, we find unequivocal traces of the Brigantes and Romans; but the frequency of the affixes, *ley, ton, den, bank, beck,* affords abundant evidence that our ancestors were chiefly Anglo-Saxon; though, in the lapse of ages, the blue-eyed Saxon race has lost its distinctiveness by intermingling with the Norman and other races. The oldest written record of their existence here which we can find, is in the following

EXTRACT FROM THE DOMESDAY SURVEY.*

THE six Manors and single Berewick, as here

---

* See Baldwin's Translation. Domesday Book is a work which was made by order of Wm. the Conqueror, about the year 1080. It contains a survey of all the estates, houses, lakes, rivers, and forests, in England; the value of every man's property, and the number of inhabitants, &c.

DOMESDAY SURVEY. 19

arranged, and which, with the exception of one, are now comprehended in the Parish of Keighley, are thus noticed in that invaluable document:—

"Manor in Utelai, (Utley) William had one carucate to be taxed.

"Two Manors in Chichleai, (Keighley) Ulchel, and Thole, and Ravensuar, and William, had six carucates to be taxed.

"Manor in Wilsedene, (Wilsden) Gamelbar had three carucates to be taxed.

"Manor in Acarde, (Oakworth) Gamelbar and William had one carucate to be taxed.

"Manor in Lacoc, (Laycock) Ravensuar had two carucates to be taxed.

"Berewick in Newhuse, (Newsholme) William had one carucate to be taxed."

We have here a list of the Saxon proprietors of the several manors as they existed in Edward the Confessor's time; which, as already stated, with the exception of Wilsden, now constitute the Parish of Keighley. But in the interval between the Conquest and termination of the great national record, Oakworth, Steeton, and many other lordships had been bestowed upon Giselbert, or Gilbert Tyson, one of the Norman followers; and Wilsden soon after passed into the hands of that powerful chief, Ilbert de Lacy,[*] and became a part of the Parish of Bradford. "The rest were Terra Regis, and by grant to Robert de Romille, soon after became part

---

[*] The ruthless Conqueror, who steeled his conscience against Yorkshire, conferred upon this adherent no less than 150 manors in the West-Riding alone. He built the castle of Pontefract for his residence and to overawe his vassals.

of the original Skipton Fee." Altogether there appears to have been eleven carucutes of land to be taxed in this parish, and as 100 to 120 acres are said to make a carucate, varying with the quality of the soil, it may be assumed that something short of 1,200 acres were at that period in some low and imperfect state of cultivation.

Of the four Saxon thanes in possession of the two manors in Keighley, and probably their ancestors, each occupied a distinct fold, or farm establishment; whilst the village, consisting chiefly of shiels, or sheds, of mud and wood, or huts of thatched wattle-work covered with mortar, which had been long gathering on the borders of the cow-field, and which still retained its original appellation, might have been their joint possession. Early, however, in the twelfth century, this town had become the property of one principal family, which had erected a church, and taken the surname—De Kygheley. This family and their noble descendants of the house of Cavendish, have remained lords of the place during the long and unbroken period of seven hundred years.

THE PARISH CHURCH.

VIEW OF THE CHURCH PRIOR TO 1805.

On a much decayed stone in the south-western angle of the old steeple, we have frequently noticed in plain and legible relief, the outward surface painted black, something like the marks or figures here represented, ᛁᛏᛁᛁ These characters, noticed in "Gent's History of Ripon, 1733," and since construed into the date 1111, had, in all probability, been changed, either by time or some officious hand, out of the old English monogram, 𝔦𝔥𝔢—the detached part above the second figure being a portion of the long stroke of the letter 𝔥. Perhaps this explanation, with a knowledge of the fact, that the Arabic numeral was not used in churches in this country for some centuries after the above-mentioned date, will be esteemed sufficient; yet it is not a little singular that these fictitious figures should seem to point to the very time, or nearly so, when the original Parish Church is supposed to have been first erected. The historian of Craven, whom we quote, says: "On this authority, therefore," (that is the authority of Ordericus) "as well as the many striking appearances of their architecture, I assign the interval between 1100 and 1135 as the first great era of church building in Craven. In this state our churches continued at least four centuries, when, either from increase of population or change of fashion, a general enlargement of their structures took place." In the corresponding angle on the north side, was to be traced the Keighley coat-of-arms, with the cross arrows, and one or two grotesque faces.

"The Church of Keighley was given, at a very early period, to the prior and canons of Bolton, by Ralph de Keighley, whose son Richard released all his rights in the said church, by a charter attested, "Rogero Tempest." It was never appropriated; and after the dissolution of monasteries, the advowson was granted, *inter alia*, to Henry Earl of Cumberland, 33rd of Henry VIII."

This Rectory was valued in Pope Nicholas's taxation, 1292, at £8. In the King's Books, 1539, at £21. 0s. 6d. At another period, viz., 1702, it is stated, as will subsequently appear, to be worth £150. a year; and in the 12th Annual Report of the Church Pastoral Aid Society, published 1847, the net annual income of the living, with the parsonage house, (in answer to certain inquiries put by the committee) is returned by the Rector as worth £420. a year. This value, it is presumed, is independent of the Easter dues and small tithes, which, in con-

THE PARISH CHURCH. 23

sequence of the fine attributes of charity and mercy prevailing more with the late and present Rector than a sense of rectorial rights, have been suffered to remain in abeyance.

"In the north aisle of this church, belonging to Riddlesden Hall, are two ancient grave-stones, each of which has a cross and a sword and two shields of arms, the higher nearly effaced, the lower charged with a cross fleury, and circumscribed: "𝔊𝔦𝔩𝔟𝔢𝔯𝔱𝔲𝔰 𝔎𝔶𝔤𝔥𝔩𝔢𝔶 𝔡𝔢 𝔄𝔱𝔩𝔞𝔶 𝔢𝔱 𝔐𝔞𝔯𝔤𝔞𝔯𝔦𝔞 𝔲𝔵𝔬𝔯𝔢𝔰, 𝔄. 𝔇. 𝔇𝔪. 1023." In "Gent's History of Ripon," the date given is 1022. The nearly effaced shield is clearly the arms of the Keighley family, before the addition of the crest, and the other shield is charged with a cross moline and crescent in middle base.*

When Dodsworth visited this church in 1621, there appears to have been no painted glass; "but a single shield in this choir, quarterly, arg. a fess, between three mullets, pierced, sab. (Paslew); 2nd, sab. a lion rampant, gules debruised, with two bars, sab. (Maud)—the same ancient ensigns having been lately copied by John Maud, Esq., a member of that family, from a window in West Riddlesden Hall; 3rd, arg. a chevron between three cross crosslets, fitchee, sab.; 4th as the first." But is it not somewhat strange that Dodsworth should have overlooked the subject of the following paragraph from Gent?

"There was a quarry of glass taken down from the great window in the east end of the church, behind the communion table, now left in the hands

---

* It is evident from the crescent on his shield that he was either a second son or the descendant of a second son. The principal branch of the Keighleys of Keighley resided either at Utley or at Inskip, near Preston, in Lancashire.

of one who was formerly sexton. It hath upon it the portraiture of a pope's head crowned with three crowns, and this inscription, spherewise, over the head—"*Bonificius ut videas in pano Christi altare posuit.*"* Boniface the eighth, probably the pontiff here intended, was elevated 1294. Boniface the ninth, and last pope of that name, died 1404.

It has been supposed, from the nature of the groundwork, that there were at one time two Chantry Chapels in this Church. The Altar here pointed out as erected under the auspices of one of the Popes Boniface, probably stood in the south choir; but by whom founded, or when discontinued, we have no evidence, recollecting only what was stated by Mr. Gale, in 1710, that, "the south aisle, by ancient writings, belonged to one Mr. Ramsden, of Braithwaite."

The following may be adduced as a purely incidental but corroborative fact. David Bastow, the third sexton of that name, whilst digging a grave close to the Church, on the south side, turned up a very ancient seal, small, but in excellent preservation, with the figure of a man kneeling before a cross, having a crescent above it, and behind, a star surrounded by the following inscription:—"S. Ricardi de Kendal Cap." It is in the old English character, without date, but certainly older than the reformation, and decidedly a relic of the 'olden times.' But who was this Richard de Kendal? Was he a chantry priest, or parson of the parish? It will be considered a strange coincidence indeed, should he be destined to make

---

* This monkish Latin is very incorrect. The best rendering seems to be, "Boniface, as thou mayst see, placed the bread of Christ upon the altar."

up another gap in our still imperfect list of Rectors—
that is, between the years 1295 and 1420.

A LIST OF RECTORS AND PATRONS.

When inducted.	RECTORS.	PATRONS.
July, 1245,	D's. W. le Vavasour, Presb.,	Prior and Canons of Bolton.
Before 1270,	Thomas Parson, of Keighley,	do.
April, 1295,	Mr. Robt. de Nassington, Subd.,	do.
	D's. Rob. de Duffield,	do.
May, 1420,	D's. Robt. Browne, Presb.,	do.
Aug. 1446,	D's. Joh. Bradford Capell, ob. 1477,	do.
	D's. Robt. Thompson, alias Darnton,	do.
Nov., 1503,	D's. Robt Mason, Presb.,	do.
April, 1524,	D's. Cristopher Ashton, Presb.,	do.
Jan., 1555.	D's. Joh. Medehope, Cl.,	Henry Earl of Cumberland.
Dec., 1572,	Antonious Forde, S. T. P.,	Collated by the Archbishop.
Jan., 1578,	Ric. Patchett, vel Paget, Cl., ob. 1615, ...	Executors of Henry Earl of Cumberland.
May, 1616,	Thomas Browne, Cl., A. M.,	Francis Earl of Cumberland.
Nov., 1636,	Francis Claver, Cl., S. T. B.,	do.
Nov., 1660,	Tho. Danby, Cl.,	Richard Earl of Cork.
May, 1675,	Jonathan Dryden, A. M.,	do.
1680,	Miles Gale, A. M.,	do.
1720—21,	Tobias Wickham,	Charles Earl of Burlington.
	Benj. Collins, M. A., ob. 1736,	Richard Earl of Burlington.
1736,	Richard Scott, ob. 1747,	do.
1747,	John Pidding, ob. 1753,	do.
1753,	Charles Knowlton, A. M.,"	do.
1814,	Theodore Dury, M. A., resigned,	William Spencer, Duke of Devonshire.
1840,	William Busfeild, M, A. and Rural Dean (the present Incumbent),	do.

Thomas Parson, of Keighley, second in the list, was met with in papers relating to Glusburn and Elslack, published in the *Collectanea Topographica et Geneologica*, he having been witness to a deed previous to the year 1270.

"Anno 1710 this church was made uniform as to the windows: the middle choir by the Parson, and the body by the Parish; and the same year beautified with fifteen compartments, which contain a short history of the blessed Jesus, the Virgin Mary, the twelve Apostles, and St. Paul, with the figure of each head set crestwise; also, old Time flying and running a skeleton, with many scripture sentences, besides the Creed, the Lord's prayer, and the ten commandments.

"The north aisle, at the east end, belongs to Riddlesden Hall, the arms of the Passlew being both on the main and on the stone, in divers places, and they having constantly repaired the same.

"The south aisle, by ancient writings, belongs to one Mr. Ramsden, of Braithwaite, who consented to the making of a vestry, providing the Parish would make him a large pew joining to the little south door; which was done." *

Had not Whitaker's real or affected dislike to manufactures been made an excuse for the neglect of duties, which as a meek divine and faithful historian he had engaged to perform, he would not, by wilful omission or contemptuous neglect, have made himself a party to an egregious blunder, committed originally, we believe, by Mr. Gale, respecting the date of the two old gravestones before mentioned. Had his keen and searching eye been directed to these, and two other ancient stones found under the groundwork of the old church, these remarks would have been uncalled for, and the present writer, whose only object is the truth, relieved from an onerous duty. Though the precise date of these sepulchral monuments cannot now be ascertained, it will require little sagacity on the part of the antiquarian reader to perceive, that 1023, assigned by one party and assented to by others, is glaringly erroneous and ab-

* Gale's Manuscript.

surd; for the Domesday Survey, taken some sixty years after this assigned date, affords a direct negative proof that there was neither church nor priest here at that time, the doctor himself, in his sceond edition of the "History of Craven," acknowledging that the only churches known to have existed before the Conquest in this district were—Long Preston, Kirby Malghdale, Kildwick, and Bernoldswick. Besides it is well known to antiquarians, that there was no such thing at that early period as family surnames amongst the Saxons. The same eminent, but biased historian, notwithstanding his silence on this occasion, in reference to the Hawksworth pedigree, in the "Ducatus Leodiensis," thus remarks: "Domesday will prove, that almost twenty years after the battle of Hastings the local surname did not exist; and it was not till two centuries after the time of Henry I. that there was a Savile of Thornhill." Again, page 128, Loidis and Elmete, in respect to the witness of a deed supposed to refer to the middle of Henry III., (1244) he observes: "Adam de Leeds, in Secroft, that is, dwelling in Secroft, affords one of the earliest instances of a local name retained after a family had migrated to another place." And in Lyson's "Cheshire Magna Britannia," it is stated that, "Armorial devices do not appear to have been introduced on works of Art in this country before the reign of Richard the First, who died 1199, nor on sepulchral monuments till the thirteenth century;" the writer further adding, "that the earliest example of armorial devices we have romaining, is that which appears on the shield of this monarch on his great seal." Should further proof be necessary, it will be found on an examination of the stone, that instead of the more ancient Saxon characters of that period, it is circumscribed with old English, probably of the fourteenth or beginning of the fifteenth century. But admitting, for the sake of argument, the above date to be correct, and that there was such a person as Gilbert Keighley, of Utley, at that time, we would ask, what had become of the family in Edward the Confessor's and the Conqueror's time? For if we turn to the extract from the Domesday Survey, it will be seen, that in the former reign, the whole of this parish belonged to five Saxon thanes, or gentlemen, without ever a surname amongst them; and prior to the close of the great national account, their land had been seized by the Conqueror, and then held in his powerful and tyrannical grasp. Though some part of the inscription is still legible, and almost entire, unfortunately the date is so far wasted away as to be quite illegible. Mr. Baines, who appears to have been the first to suspect this glaring and preposterous anachronism, has the following remark: "This date, if the cyphers have not been defaced by time or accident, and restored by some careless hand, refers to the reign of Canute, and few of our churches can boast a sepulchral monument of so remote a period."*

One of the two ancient grit stones discovered on taking up the foundation of the old church, is five feet six inches long, having the general appearance of a stone coffin, surrounded by a moulding and upon it there are two plain crosses, with another common emblem, the pincers, which, with the hammer and nails, were formerly used to represent the

---

Gilbert Keighley was living in 1380, and dead in 1384.

sufferings of Christ on the cross. The other stone is about the same length but a little narrower, being only fourteen inches wide, and on it are two parallel lines 2¼ inches apart, crowned by four annulets 3¼ in diameter, and the lower two are about one inch from the tops of the parallel lines.* They were probably the foundation, or corner stones, of some former edifice; and the inscribed crosses were evidently designed to symbolize the cross of Christ as the only foundation of the true church. Of the meaning of the annulets there is some uncertainty. Dr. Whitaker informs us, in his "History of Craven," that an old stone was lately found at Embsay marked with the annulets, which he supposes to have been an ancient boundary-stone of the Viponts. This throws but little light on the subject; whether a branch of the Keighley family bore annulets as a charge in their coat of arms, or added them as a difference, and wishful to perpetuate the circumstance, had them engraven on this stone, we know not. If they are not of heraldic import, may we not conceive them to be emblems of the eternal affinity existing between the church, as bride, and the Lord Jesus Christ, as bridegroom?

This church, though dedicated to St. Peter, is sometimes claimed on the part of St. Andrew; the partizans of the Scottish saint deriving their authority from Mr. Baines, and he, probably from the communication of an unknown correspondent in Gent's "History of Ripon," who, without producing the slightest evidence, observes; "The feast of the

---

* In a drawing of this stone, made by order of J. A. Busfeild, Esq., Upwood, the artist has, by mistake, disarranged the rings, by making the upper and lower acute angles formed by lines joining their centres too small, and connected the two lower to the tops of the parallel lines.

town is kept on St. Peter's Day, but the church is dedicated to St. Andrew;" the Peterites relying on Dr. Whitaker, and the Doctor on Mr. Gale's manuscript. The last-named gentleman, who was Rector of this parish from 1680 to 1721, says, "I suppose the church to be dedicated to St. Peter, because the feast is held on St. Peter's day." This is the popular opinion at the present time; and we think that no stronger evidence need be required. Dr. Burns, however, states that, "Wherever Sunday wakes are guided by a foregoing festival, we may be justly satisfied the church was dedicated to the saint of that day." Since the establishment of the new or May fair, the feast of the town has been confined to the village of Utley; and the inhabitants, rigidly adhering to ancient custom, on a late occasion could not be prevailed upon, even for their own convenience, to defer the festival of their patron saint to the following Sunday. Besides the altar, dedicated to Christ, as before intimated, it has been supposed that our Parish Church contained, at an early period, a chantry chapel and altar dedicated to St. Andrew, and that the mistake about the patron saint arose out of some vague tradition of the circumstance. If such was the case, it probably occupied the site in the old church, subsequently taken up by the Starkey or Riddlesden Hall pew, commonly called the North Choir.

January 30th, 1761, a license was granted to erect a gallery at the west end of the church; and in the same year, the old peal of three bells, was exchanged for a musical peal of six.

VIEW OF THE CHURCH PRIOR TO 1846.

In 1805, this church was entirely rebuilt at the expense of the parishioners, after the style represented in the above view. From the lower part of the old tower, supposed to have been erected in the early part of Elizabeth's reign, and composed of sound moor stone, strengthened by well-graduated buttresses, was made to spring something designated a steeple, of an octagonal form, covered with a dome of lead, and surmounted by a ponderous weathercock. At the same time two additional bells were put up, and soon after an organ was raised by a private subscription. A new church-clock was also added, which is accounted a curious and accurate piece of workmanship, and described in several treatises on clock and watch work. It was made by John Prior, of Nessfield, in Wharfedale, (commonly called the Yorkshire Mechanic) after the tedious course of seven years. The striking part was his own invention, and the escapement the invention of his son, Mr. George Prior, of Leeds. It shows the hours and minutes on four dials, striking the hours and quarters.

The Organ, as already stated, was raised by subscription, in the year 1811, the Rev. Charles Knowlton being Rector, and John Spencer, senior, George Richardson, William Newsholme, and William Smith, Churchwardens. The subjoined is a list of the subscribers' names, with the amount of their several subscriptions, taken (in 1842) from the memorial which is now behind the new organ.

	£.	s.		£.	s.
"Messrs. Wm. Clayton & Son	35	10	John Greenwood, Esq.	31	10
Messrs. John Spencer & Sons	31	10	Lister Ellis, Esq.	20	0
William Sugden, Esq.	20	0	Mr. Thomas Delefare	5	5
Mr. Samuel Blakey	20	0	,, Thomas Rhodes	5	5
William Ellis, Esq.	10	10	,, John Ramsden	5	5
Mrs. Marrinet	10	10	,, Joseph Heaton	5	5
Mr. John Blakey	10	10	,, Joseph Padget	5	5
,. Joseph Emmett	10	10	,, Samuel Wignall	5	5
,, Thomas Smith	10	10	,, Benj. Blackborough	5	5
,, Richard Williamson	10	10	,, Joshua Cowling	5	5
,, Thomas Binns	10	10	,, Richard Hattersley	5	5
,, Thomas Corlass	10	10	,, Abraham Binns	5	5
,, Robert Dawson	10	10	,, Henry Lister	5	5
,, George Richardson	10	10	Trustees of the Methodists' Chapel	5	16
,, Berry Smith	10	10	Mr. Michael Merrall	3	3
Messrs. John Taylor & Sons	10	10	,, John Walker	3	3
Mr. William Newsholme	8	8	,, William Beecroft	3	3
Mrs. Elizabeth Smith	5	5	,, Thomas Dawson	3	3
Mr. Richard Hollings	5	5	,, John Allen	1	1
,, William Cockshott	5	5	,, Thomas Thompson	1	1
., William Illingworth	5	5	,, John Peel	1	1
,, John Ellison	5	5	,, James Smith	1	1
,, Robert Sugden	1	1	£400	11"	

All lovers of 'Old Methodism' will be pleased to see this list preserved, because it shows that Mr.

CHARITIES.

Wesley's attachment to the church of England was strongly reflected by his followers here, in their individual and official contributions.

"A Record of Benefactions in the Parish of Keighley, Miles Gale, A. M., being Rector, 1713." [Copied, in 1842, from the table now in the west part of the tower.]

"Isabel Hall, of Keighley, by deed, February 24th, 1633, gave £1. per annum, to be distributed by the Minister and Churchwardens to the poor of Keighley on St. Matthias's day.

"Isaac Bowcock, of Tong, Stapler, by will, February 11th, 1669, gave to this Parish £4. per annum out of Lands in Utley; also £21. per annum lying in Bradford, for these uses:—1st, Putting out five poor men's sons apprentices. 2nd, Supplying the wants of those in necessity, and not relieved by the Parish. 3rd, Setting in trade and stock such as are hopeful.*

"George Clapham, of Exleyhead, gave by will, April 23rd, 1681, to relieve such as have of the Poor Cess, £1. per annum, to be distributed by the Minister and Churchwardens on St. Thomas's day.

"John Clapham, of Weethead, gave by will, dated October 26th, 1686, out of Lands at Ingrow-wood, £1. 16s. per annum, to be distributed by the Minister and Churchwardens on St Thomas's day.

"John Drake, by will, March 27th, 1713, gave all his Lands and Buildings, in Keighley, towards the maintenance of a Schoolmaster, for instructing the children of the town and parish of Keighley aforesaid, in the

---

* Mr. Bowcock, whose bounteous hand was also extended to Halifax, Ovenden, and Colne, was the son of George Bowcock, baptized at Keighley, 1596.

English, Latin, and Greek tongues without any other reward.

"Mr. John Green, in the Parish of St. Saviour's, in the County of Surrey, gave £100., to be settled on a good and sure Freehold Estate of inheritance, for and towards the said Free School, so settled, or intended to be settled, by the said John Drake, in the sure and good foundation for the purpose for ever. November, 1715.

"Mr. Jonas Tonson, of Exleyhead, in the Parish of Keighley, in the County of York, left (1716) £100. to be settled on a good and sure Freehold Estate of inheritance, for and towards the said Free School, for an Usher in the sure and good foundation for ever.

"Sarah Heaton, of Deanfield, in the Parish of Keighley, left the interest of £200. for ever, towards the maintenance of a Schoolmaster at Harehill, in the Parish aforesaid, 1743."

In 1808,—the year when the original table was copied over, and the time, as one would have supposed, when Jonas Tonson and Sarah Heaton's Bequests ought to have been added, the annual value is thus stated:—

		£.	s.	d.
"Annual value of John Drake's Charity		70	0	0
,,	John Green's do.	4	0	0
,,	Isabel Hall's do.	5	5	0
,,	Isaac Bowcock's do.	113	17	0
,,	George Clapham's do.	5	5	0
,,	John Clapham's do.	12	1	0
Rent of the Poor's Allotment to be distributed on St. Matthias's day		2	12	6"

In 1853, Bowcock's Charity was about £320.; Drake's, £160.; and the Poor's Estate, about £30. a year.

It might have been supposed that this church, which had cost upwards of £4000., besides a great sum in alterations and repairs, would at least have sufficed for a few generations. But this was not the case. The wretched stuff of which the roof had been constructed was found to be in a state of decay, whilst the moistened plaster had begun to drop from the ceiling, and this, as it happened, when four Ecclesiastical Districts were to be carved out of the Parish, and four new churches built. The Episcopalian party, alive to the importance of so critical a conjuncture, and convinced, as it seems, of the responsibilities attached to wealth, determined, in 1840, to have the fabric substantially and entirely rebuilt, on a scale in some degree commensurate with the wants of a rapidly increasing population, But it was not until the 24th of February, 1846, that the foundation of the present edifice was laid. This ceremony was performed by Frederick Greenwood, Esq., one of the principal subscribers. An address was delivered by the Rev. W. Busfeild, M.A., the Rector, and a sermon preached on the occasion, in St. John's Church, by the Hon. and Rev. Philip York Saville, M.A. So that within the compass of about forty-three years, and still in the recollection of hundreds of the parishioners, three churches have stood upon the same foundation,—a circumstance probably unparalleled in the annals of church building in this country.

The present Parish Church, as before intimated, was raised by voluntary contributions, from designs by R. D. Chantrell, F.S.A., at the cost of nearly £7000., and is calculated to accommodate 1400 hearers. The style is the Perpendicular English which prevailed in the early Tudors, and is so called from the perpendicular character of the tracery of the windows and other details in it. The Consecration, by Thomas Lord Bishop of Ripon, took place August 11th, 1848, St. John's having been used as the Parish Church during the interim. A good description of this beautiful edifice is given in a tract, published by T. D. Hudson, and entitled, "Consecration of the Parish Church of St. Andrew's, Keighley." The old organ has been replaced this year (1857) by a new one, of the value of £320.

THE RECTORY.

The Rectory, or Parsonage House, which was an unsightly heap of stones and mortar, sheltered on the north by the old tithe-barn, appears to have been considerably repaired by Mr. Gale, whose name we remember to have seen on the court entry. Mr. Pidding, the fourth in succession from him, after having determined to have it rebuilt, died when part of the stones were already hewn, and some progress made with the work; but Mr. Knowlton, probably unable to carry out the design, suffered the stones to be taken away and used for other purposes, and no other attempt was made until the arrival of Mr. Dury, who succeeded in raising the present edifice. The old house stood lower down in the field, surrounded by some fine old trees, which were cut down, and the present ground laid out and planted.

ST. JOHN'S CHURCH.

The first stone of the new church, dedicated to St. John the Evangelist, was laid on the 2nd of August,

ST. JOHN'S CHURCH.

1841, by the Rev. William Busfeild, M.A., Rector of this parish, and an address delivered on the occasion by his late venerable and highly respected father, the Rev. Johnson Atkinson Busfeild, D.D., brother of the late William Busfeild, Esq., M.P. for Bradford, and uncle to William Busfeild Ferrand, Esq., late M.P. for the Borough of Knaresborough. This district* comprises the southern vicinity of the town, and a rural part of the parish of Keighley, with Hainworth manor, in the parish of Bingley, and is denominated the District of Ingrow-cum-Hainworth. The church cost about £2000., which was raised by subscription, and the following grants:—The Parliamentary Commissioners, £500.; the Church Building Society, £400.; and the Ripon Diocesan Society, £300. The site of the church and churchyard was the gift of the Earl of Burlington. Mr. Rawsthorne, of Bradford, was the architect. During the building of the Parish Church, St. John's was used in its stead; the duties of the latter place having been performed by the Rector, until the induction of the Rev. W. G. Mayne, M.A., the present minister, in November, 1846. The living is only £50. per annum, derived from the ecclesiastical commissioners; it is in the patronage of the Bishop of Ripon.

The school, in connexion with this church, was erected in 1844, from designs by Mr. Wallen, of Huddersfield. At the census of 1851, the district contained 4020 inhabitants, 1676 of which resided in Keighley, and 2344 in Bingley parish. A neat and eligibly situated parsonage, in the domestic Gothic style of architecture, was erected in 1852.

---

* These Districts have, by Lord Blandford's Act of 1856, become New Parishes for all ecclesiastical purposes.

ST. MARY'S CHURCH.

The friends of the Anglican Church may well rejoice at the completion of the third of the four additional new churches required to meet the spiritual wants of the parish, in accordance with its re-division, evincing, as it does, her great inherent strength and energies to be paramount to all difficulties. The entire outlay on ecclesiastical and school buildings in this parish, during the last 16 years, amounts to no less a sum than £16,000. Verily, "She hath done what she could."

The licensed room in the Eastwood district has been superseded by the erection of a neat little church, in the early English style of architecture, and dedicated to St. Mary the Virgin. It has 508 sittings, and a good organ; cost £2057., exclusive of the ground, which was given by the munificent Earl of Burlington, and it was consecrated by the Lord Bishop of Ripon in June, 1855. The living is a perpetual curacy, valued at £150. per annum, and in the alternate gift of the crown and the Bishop of Ripon. This district, containing a population of 3500 persons, was constituted under Sir Robert Peel's Act, in 1844, out of a portion of the south east of the town and parish, and an adjoining slip of Bingley parish. The Rev. J. Room, B.A., the present Incumbent, succeeded the late Rev. Timothy Brayshaw, M.A., author of "Metrical Mnemonics," who died in 1854.

A school and master's house are in course of building, on the same plot of ground, at the estimated cost of £960.

THE KING'S MILL AND CONSOLIDATED MANORS.

In 1710, Laycock and Utley, two of the five Domesday manors, appear to have been so completely absorbed into that of Keighley, as to have left no traces of their once distinct and separate existence, otherwise they could not have been overlooked by Mr. Gale at that time, nor by a subsequent writer in 1733, who has left us the following account:—

"There are three manors in this parish. The first belongs to His Grace the Duke of Devonshire; the second to the Lord Fairfax, of Denton, within five miles of this place; the third to Mr. Michael Stell, of Well Head, in this parish, who lately died, and since his disease, it fell to his eldest son and heir, Mr. Michael Stell, of Well Head, in the parish of Keighley. In all which are or may be kept Courts Baron, though only in the first there is kept a three weeks' Court on a Thursday, and two head Court days in a year."*

Thwaites, which was next doomed to be drawn into the absorbing vortex, was sold by Thomas Baron Fairfax, some time previous to 1739, and there being little or no waste or common right, the necessity for holding courts ceased to exist, and the freeholders, probably feeling no further interest in the matter, quietly suffered this small but ancient lordship to coalesce with Keighley.

Although Whitaker, in his "History of Craven," 1811, treats Thwaites as a distinct manor, it may be said to have been finally incorporated with the rest thirty or forty years previous to that time.

---
* Gent's History of Ripon.

The four consolidated manors now belong to William Cavendish, second Earl of Burlington (of that name,) whose steward claims for the Manor Courts of Keighley, with the exception of Oakworth, the right of jurisdiction throughout the whole parish. The Courts are held at the Devonshire Arms once a year, for the presentation of Nuisances, appointing the Bellman, Pinder, and other business; and every three weeks, if necessary, for the recovery of debts under £5. Charles Carr, Esq., of Skipton, is Steward, and John Hopkinson, Bailiff. It appears that the interests of this Court were formerly much neglected, for we are informed that a lawyer's clerk, of the name of Peel, in the employ of the late Mr. Watson, was suffered to purloin or embezzle a part of the Court Rolls. But let us put musty deeds aside, while we treat our younger readers to a little gossip about the feats of a newly-appointed Pinder and Jerry Wells's Goose.

"At the County Court of Keighley, held last week, (Jan. 12th, 1853) his Honour had a little sunshine thrown over the usual dull routine of his business, by the eccentricities of Jerry Wells's Goose. This well-known bird, which he had bought and nourished up, and which 'ate of his own meat, and drank of his own cup, and was the sole comfort of his declining years,' one unlucky morning was kidnapped by the Pinder, who had been newly appointed by the Court Leet of Keighley. Now the Pinder, being a man without a particle of romance in his composition, and with no redundancy of the finer feelings of our nature, determined unflinchingly to do his duty, and Jerry Wells's poor solitary goose, that had for a long time enlivened the neighbourhood with its cackle, was, according to the phraseology of the Pinder, 'clapt it pinfold.'

Jerry being advised officially of the state of things, refused to 'fork out,' and the poor goose was left in durance vile. The following morning not a cackle was heard, or a feather seen; the goose was gone. Whether it was stolen, or whether feeling indignant at being placed in a low neighbourhood, it had departed of its own accord, did not transpire; but Jerry Wells was minus a goose, so sued the Pinder for damages in the County Court. The Pinder, on finding himself assailed, called up his reserves to the rescue, and the Court Leet of the Earl of Burlington, represented by Mr. Carr, of Skipton, and Mr. Carrodus, the High Bailiff, debouched into the field, and put the battle in array against the plaintiff and his goose. The turning-point appeared to be the right and authority of Billy Speak, the Pinder, to take the goose. Billy cited as his authority, Mr. Stell, a Churchwarden, who had advised him to take it; and he also called upon the High Bailiff to produce the records of the Court, and search for precedents. Mr. Carrodus, who had been High Bailiff a considerable part of the present half-century, and knew all about geese, produced the records, and found a precedent in the reign of Queen Anne. Billy also insinuated that the goose was a consenting party. All these points having been ably discussed, the Court ordered the plaintiff to be nonsuited. Had the goose been present, the case might have ended differently; but as the bird proved an alibi, its master was left in the lurch."

The duties of this Court are now little more than nominal.

"Nigh the town, upon one of the brooks, is a King's Mill, which by lease yields £44. 13s. 4d. rent per annum, out of which is paid a free rent of £3. 2s.

per annum, to Mr. Thomas Layton, of Rawden, in the parish of Guiseley, five miles from hence." * The prescribed limits of the King's Mill, or soke, was probably determined soon after the formation of the parish, though not coextensive with it, including only Keighley, Longlee, Utley, and Thwaites. The tradition still exists of the two latter places having to furnish wood and stone for repairs, in return for the privilege of grinding, or what was then termed hopper-right; and in wills, and other legal documents, property in Longlee, Thwaites, or Utley, is generally described as within Keighley (that is, within the soke of Keighley), but beyond a certain line westward, as in the parish of Keighley. The Laytons, as we shall perceive hereafter, became entitled to the above-named free-rent, by marriage with a branch of the Keighley family.

THE MARKET, FAIRS, AND FREE WARREN.

In 1305, a charter was obtained by Henry Keighley, securing to himself and heirs the privilege of a Market, Fair, and Free Warren, within the manor of Keighley. This gentleman was "Steward and Master Forester of Blackburnshire, under the great Earl of Lincoln," through whose influence the charter was procured from Edward the First, one of the greatest and most magnanimous of our English Kings. Five years after the date of this charter, we find the following to be the market prices of the articles mentioned :— wheat, 6s. a quarter; oats, 3s.; eggs, ½d. a dozen; ale, ½d. a gallon; a cow, 12s. 6d.; a sheep, 1s. 2d.; a fat pig, 3s. 4d.; a fat goose, 2½d.; a pair of shoes,

---

* Gale's Manuscript.

4d.; a labourer's wages, 1½d. a day, in harvest time, 2d.; a journeyman carpenter, 2d. a day; a riding horse, 13s. 4d.; an English slave and his family sold for 13s. 4d.; a bible, £33. 6s. 8d.

On this subject we meet with the following passage in Gibson's edition of Camden:—

"The Aire, having passed Craven, is carried in a much larger channel, with pleasant fields on both sides, by Kighley, from which the famous family of Kighley derive their name, one of whom, Henry Kighley (interred here), procured from Edward the First, for this his manor, the privileges of a Market, a Fair, and Free Warren, so that none might enter into these grounds to chase therein, with a design to catch any thing pertaining to the said warren, without the permission and leave of the said Henry and his successors. This was a very considerable favour in those days, and we the rather take notice of it because it teaches us the nature and meaning of a Free Warren. The male issue in the right line of this family ended in Henry Kighley, of Inskip, within the memory of the present age.* The daughters and heirs were married, one to William Cavendish, then Baron Cavendish, of Hardwick; the other, to Thomas Worsley, of Booths."

The reader may smile at the importance attached to Free Warren; but in those days, the gentry and nobility were passionately fond of the chase. For instance, Archbishop Melton, accounted a good and charitable person, at his visitation to Bolton, Kildwick, Embsay, and other places, in 1321, hunted, with a pack of hounds, in his progress from parish to parish. Wolves, occasionally the objects of pursuit, though rare,

---
* This was sold 1607

were not extinct in Craven. The last wolf in Airedale is said to have fallen near Leeds, in a hunt by John O'Gaunt, Duke of Lancaster, who died, 1399.

The old Fair, according to the charter, was held on the 27th of October, and when changed, by the alteration of the style, to the 8th of November, another Fair was attempted to be established, which, meeting with the approbation and support of the neighbourhood, continues to be held on the 8th of May. The Market, after having been held on the Church-Green for more than five centuries, was removed to its present site in the month of November, 1833. It was raised by a company of shareholders, and is held by lease of the Earl of Burlington. The old market-cross was removed in the latter part of the last century, in order to make room for the opening into Skipton road, now North-street. Wednesday is the chartered market, but Saturday is becoming the principal market-day. To this ancient charter (a copy of which was procured and put in evidence on the late trial to prove the lord's right to remove the market) is appended the following list of highly distinguished witnesses:—

> "William, Bishop of Coventry and Lichfield.
> Henry de Lacy, Earl of Lincoln.
> Humphrey de Bohun, Earl of Hereford and Essex.
> Ralphe de Monte Heimer,
> John de Brittan.
> Aymer de Valence, Earl of Pembroke.
> Hugh de Lespencer, Earl of Winchester.
> R. de la Ward, Steward of the Household."

It will be observed, that the market was held on the Church-Green, in close proximity to the church-yard, but never within it, as was the profane custom of many towns; and it is congratulatory to find that the market was never held on a Sunday, as was the case at Bradford and other places.

The Park was probably paled or fenced round on the reception of this charter, its situation and extent being still ascertainable eastward of the town, in the fields called 'The Parks,' 'Broad Parks,' Park Wood, and Park-lane. The names of the 'Park' and the 'Paddock' being, so far as we know, the only existing mementos of one dominant influential family having once resided in the town; even the site of the manor-house appears to have been long since forgotten. But in a note appended to a pedigree of the Keighleys, transcribed from the Harleian manuscripts, and communicated to the Archæological Institute, by J. A. Busfeild, Esq., there is the following very curious notice of the ancient residence of the lords of this manor:—" I then inquired for the Manor-house of Keighley, belonging to this family, and was shown a poor cottage, where a simple schoolmaster lived, where, they informed me, stood formerly the hall and great large buildings, but now converted into meadows, orchards, and gardens." The writer of this, I believe, is not known, but the date, 1667, renders it exceedingly interesting.

As this Sir Henry Keighley thrice represented Lancashire in parliament, it is not improbable that he would be one of the members, who this year complained to the King, that coals were so generally used that the air was infected; in consequence of which, two proclamations were issued prohibiting their further use in the metropolis, and containing strict orders to inflict fines, and destroy all furnaces and kilns where coal fires should be found. This strikingly illustrates the power of prejudice, and the slowness of the public mind to admit and appreciate great discoveries. We may reasonably infer that wood and peat would be the only fuel consumed here at this period.

FLODDEN FIELD.

A LIST of individuals from the different townships in Craven, who in 1513, followed the Lord Clifford, and fought under the standard of the Earl of Surrey at the battle of Flodden Field, was, a few years ago, transcribed by the Rev. Wm. Carr, of Bolton, probably from the ancient muster-roll, preserved in the archives of the descendants of the Cliffords. This list was presented to John Nicholson, and added to the poem of "Airedale." The following being the names of the individuals from the parish of Keighley, who shared in the honours of that decisive victory:—

"John Rawson, bow, horse and harness.
Lawrence Ambler, bow, able horse and harness.
Ellis Hall, bow.
John Butterfield, bill.
Richard Rycroft, bill.
John Netherwood, bill.
Edward Rawson, bow.
Robert Bottomley, bow.
Richard Shaw, bow.
Robert Lupton, bill.
Ellis Wadsworth, bill.
William Roper, bill.
William Farnhill, bill.
Robert Stell, bill.
William Jackson, bow.
John Hanson, bow.
Robert Rawson, bow.
Edward Moore, bow.
Richard Shackylton, bow.
Thomas Stotte, bow.
Richard Jenkinson, bow.
William Eastburn, bill.
Richard Frythyll, bow.
William Denby, bill.
William Sugden, bill.
John Clough, bill.
William Smith, bill.
William Butterfield, bow.
Xrofer Ruddying, bow.
John Shaw, bow.
John Brigg, bill,
John Stotte, bow.
Thomas Lakok, bill.
Richard Sharppe, bow.
John Weddoppe, bow.
James Proctor, bow.
Robert Sugden, Bow.
John Oldfield, bow.
John Wedhope, bow.
Henry Beanlands, bow.
Thomas Sowden, bill.
John Cockroft, bow.
Robert Wright, bow.
Robert Wright, junior, bow.
William Hartley, bow.
Robert Hudson, bow.
John Sugden, bow.

We can best appreciate a blessing when deprived of it, or when it is contrasted with an opposite evil ; but as it would be too dearly bought experience to be deprived of the blessings of peace for the sake of increasing our love for it, let us for a moment intensify that love by a recital of one atrocious example among a thousand, incident to the ferocious wars of the 15th and 16th centuries. This Lord Clifford, who summoned his feudatories of Keighley and the neighbouring places to his service, is said to have been hid among the mountains of Cumberland, and brought up as a shepherd during the twenty-four years' ascendancy of the house of York, in consequence of the following act committed by his father. At the close of the battle of Wakefield, Dec. 31st, 1460, where the Duke of York was defeated and slain, Lord Clifford, one of the Red Rose victors, overtook a boy, richly dressed, attended by a single companion, and in full flight. "Who is this ?" exclaimed the fierce baron. "Spare his life," replied the attendant, who was his tutor, "he is the son of a prince, and may one day requite the favour." "Is it so ?" shouted Clifford. "Thy father slew my father, and thus will I slay thee and all of thy kin." As he spoke he plunged his dagger into the boy's heart, who fell dead at his feet ! The boy was the Duke of York's son.

Though none of the Keighley family are to be found in the train of the Lord Clifford at this time, it will subsequently appear that the veteran warrior, Sir Henry, fought under the same standard, and took a distinguished part in that memorable engagement. John Rawson, who went mounted and armed to the battle-field, was of the Rawsons of Stubbing House, a family of respectable yeomen or gentlemen, who resided there for many generations. We are informed in James's "History of Bradford," that "Joseph Field, Esq. of Shipley, Lord of the manor of Heaton, bap. 1601, married, 1625, Mary, eldest daughter and co-heir of William Rawson, of Bracken Bank, in the parish of Keighley; by that lady, who outlived him and died a widow, he had issue at his death in 1660. The last person of this ancient family residing in the neighbourhood, was one Thomas Rawson, who, stript of his property, like many a greater man in exigence, took to the profession of a school-master. He was engaged in this vocation, in the town, about 70 years ago. It is worthy of note that, from a collateral branch of this family, have descended the present Countess' of Rosse and the Hon. Lady Delia Duncombe.

MILITARY OCCUPATION OF THE TOWN.

Though uninformed by the local historian as to the state of this neighbourhood during the sanguinary conflict of the Roses, it will be found that the former obscurity of the town did not exempt it from a share of the civil broils of the country in the time of Charles the First, for we have it recorded by Vicars and Whitelock, "That early in the month of February, 1645, a party of about 150 horse from Skipton, taking advantage of the absence of Col. Brandling, who commanded, fell suddenly upon the Parliamentary quarters at Keighley, where they surprised the guards, got into the town, and took near a hundred prisoners, sixty horse and other booty. Col. Lambert and his party, however, who happened to be quartered in the neighbourhood, having heard of the alarm, came to their relief, and

MILITARY OCCUPATION OF THE TOWN. 49

performed their part so gallantly that they recovered all the parliamentary prisoners and most of the booty which the enemy had taken, killed fifteen of them on the spot, took about twenty prisoners, wounded and took the commander—a Captain Hughes—killed his Lieutenant also, and pursued the rest to the gates of Skipton. On Mr. Lambert's side were lost in this service, Captain Salmon, one of his best officers, and eight dragoons."

There had been some skirmishing previous to this time; for the parish register furnishes the information that a soldier was found slain on the Peat Moor, and two others buried in 1643. Again, a soldier of Colonel Cromwell's regiment was buried, and four slain, 1644, and Humphrey Bland, a soldier, was buried. All this seems to have taken place before 1645, the year when the above battle is said to have been fought. Indeed, we feel convinced that the whole affair must have taken place before '45; for, on taking an aggregate of deaths for the year, we find that in 1644 they amounted to 86, whilst in the succeeding year they were only 26, though eight of these are stated to have died of the plague. The following extract from the parish register of Skipton settles the date of this transaction beyond a doubt:—
"1644, December 31st, Major John Hughes, a most valiant soldier buried." [*] As might have been supposed, from the hostility of the party in possession of the town, the national church did not escape scot-free. The whole of the communion service probably disappeared at that time. Be this as it may, a small cup appears to have been raised by subscription amongst

---

[*] Whitaker's History of Craven.

the parishioners soon after the Restoration, embellished with the Keighley coat-of-arms, and another sacramental vessel was presented by a Lady Burlington,—probably, Juliana, the Countess Dowager, a benefactress to the parish church of Leeds.

Guard-house, now the residence of John Brigg, Esq., Magistrate, appears to have taken its name at this time from some buildings having been appropriated to the purpose. It had certainly taken its name prior to the first Scotch rebellion, and it may be considered a suitable situation for a soldier's guardroom, standing, as it does, on elevated ground a little above the town.

THORESBY'S VISIT TO THIS TOWN, 1702.

To the eminent Leeds Antiquary, who in 1702 visited this place on his way to Townley Hall, the reader is indebted for the subjoined remarks.

"We rode through part of the populous parish of Bingley, in which are the seats of Mr. Benson, of Wrenthorpe, near Wakefield, who is also lord of the manor of Bingley; Mr. Ferrand, a Justice of Peace; Mr. Busfeild, of Rishworth. Thence, through Morton to Riddlesden, the seat of Mr. Edmund Starkie, where we parted with the pleasant and populous wapontake of Skireoke, and having passed the river Aire, we entered upon Staincliffe, and lodged at Kighley, anciently the seat of a famous family of the same name, of whom Sir Henry Kighley lies buried in the church, but the date of his death not legible. One of the heiresses was married to the Lord Cavendish; and the Duke of Devonshire is the patron of the living, reputed worth £150. per annum. We lodged with the modest, good parson, Mr. Gale, who has made some curious mathematical instruments, and drawn some good figures with Indian ink, being an ingenious and obliging person. September 1st, retired (for private devotion) but, alas! too frequently prevented in the evenings for want of convenient privacy upon our journeys. Had good Mr. Gale's company about two hours. He showed us a Free School, lately erected by Mr. John Drake, of Kighley, now living, who will settle the whole of his estate upon it at death. We rode about five miles over the hills in Kighley parish, till we entered Lancashire at a heap of stones as a boundary, having on the left hand, Haworth, a church or chapel within the vicarage of Bradford, though at so great a distance as the skirts of Lancashire, where nothing appears for many miles but hills and rivulets descending to the dales." *

FURTHER EXTRACTS FROM MR. GALE'S MANUSCRIPT.

" In the year 1695, when an account was required to be taken of all the inhabitants, there appeared to be in the parish, 1704, whereof 112 are freeholders, which catalogue is kept in the vestry.

The town of Keighley contains 100 houses, and is pleasantly situated in a low valley surrounded with hills, from one of which above Hainworth, I have seen Pendle Hill, Penigent, and Ingleborough, all of which are within twenty-five miles.

" 'Tis in the midway between Bradford and Skip-

---

* Thoresby's Diary and Correspondence, edited by the Rev. Joseph Hunter. F.S.A.

ton, six miles from each," [the reader needs not be told that the old customary miles are here meant] "at the meeting of two brooks, that, running a mile further, joins with the river Aire whose head is twelve miles north-west, at a place called Malham Cove. It affords dares, oumers, minnows, perches, eels, gudgeons; and salmon, when out of season, come up to the town at Michaelmas, when poor people begin to catch them with blazing iron forks. Here are Otters, which we suppose to be fed on muscles, because the shells are generally found empty.

"A spring, that never fails, begins a mile to the west above the town, and is raised in stone troughs through the chief streets, so that almost every house has water at a small distance.

"A traveller through this parish shall not meet with half a mile of level ground, only at the east end of the town is a field of plain earth, containing $114\frac{3}{4}$ days' work, round which horse races are sometimes made. I have seen an old horse run, with ten men at certain distances, delivering of a handkerchief one to another, when the horse lost. At another time, a horse with twenty men, when the men lost. At another time, a galloway being matched with a large horse to run this course round ten times without heats, the owner of the horse not daring to run, the galloway ran by itself, which was fifteen miles; the course once round being $1\frac{1}{2}$ miles.

"The poor of the parish are numerous, and maintained by assessment, which sometimes amounts to £140. a year, besides many private gifts."

To the anonymous writer in the "History of Ripon," who appears to have been a more skilful professor of the *gentle art*, the curious observer of the finny tribes may feel obliged for having corrected the Parson's list of fish. We are told by him, that "It affords dares, gralings, menards, bonestrickles, perch, eels, gudgeons, ruff, chub, trout, salmon, and salmon smelts. The salmon, when out of season, come up the river to spawn, and return into the saltwater again. There is plenty of miller's-thumb and pike, which the river was first stored with by Mr. Tempest's fish-pond, of Broughton, breaking into the river."

The intelligent angler of the present day will be best able to point out the changes that have taken place in the species and variety of fish since 1733, the time when this catalogue was taken; but we are given to understand, that in this part of the river there are now neither oumer, gralings, ruff, salmon, nor salmon smelts, and that dares are but seldom caught; whilst in their stead, there are abundance of roach, and some cray-fish. The cause of the extinction of salmon and salmon-smelts is well known. The bursting of a gentleman's fish-pond into the canal is said to have been the means of introducing the roach; and the cray-fish are known to have been first introduced by the Garforths into a small brook near Steeton.

The "field of plain earth," sometimes used as a race-ground was the Townfield, long since divided amongst the freeholders, and now in a high state of cultivation where it has not been encroached upon by modern buildings.

THE FREE GRAMMAR SCHOOL.

THE manuscript left by Mr. Gale contains little to our purpose, being chiefly taken up with an account of the difference between himself and the rest of the trustees, ostensibly about the form and size of the building, but in reality concerning the choice of the school-master. Young Beanlands was the favourite of Mr. Gale, whilst Robert Hall, who was the leader of the parish trustees, "had a son of his own, a clergyman, and likely to want a situation." The difference, having existed nearly three years, was finally settled by the death of Mr. Hall. We cannot suppose this singular MS., called "A History of the Free Grammar School," was ever intended for public inspection, it being freely interlarded with strong invective and vulgar personal abuse, more calculated to injure than promote good morals, yet as it is now no longer private property, and as some redeeming traits of character shine through the severe language, we subjoin a few explanatory extracts which, as matter of history, may be considered not inapplicable to the subject.

"The town of Kighley having no school, nor any encouragement for promoting humane learning, whereby for want of knowledge some were seduced by that vile sect of the Quakers, and others by that wicked crew of the Anabaptists, to follow false ways of worship. It being taken into consideration by John Drake, an Innkeeper, at the Church Gate, he was resolved to break the ice in that unknown passage to the land of knowledge, hoping that others would follow his example, and not be afraid to venture them-

GRAMMAR SCHOOL. 55

selves and vessels where he led the way. Accordingly, he left a yearly salary for a Master of this Free School, under these limitations, that he should be learned as to the Latin and Greek tongues, also, to be master so long as he continues unmarried. What the salary is, will be known when we come to write of his life and death. His requiring a master who was able to teach Latin and Greek, showed that he designed it for a Grammar School, so that the feoffees should be false to their trust, if they only set up a petty one for teaching English. What remains, after the payment of the funeral expenses, probate of the will, debts, and legacies, is to go to the further improvement of the master's income."

Mr. Drake's epitaph may be introduced here, as affording an example of our author's poetical talent. He died May 23rd, 1713, and was buried inside the church, and the lines upon his gravestone are still legible.

> "Here lies the body of John Drake,
> Who never did his friends forsake;
> Houses and lands he left to be
> A Free School Master's salary;
> He lived and died without a mate,
> And yielded to the laws of fate."

"He appointed seven Feoffees, who are these, 1st, Milo Gale; 2nd, Robert Hall; 3rd, Jonas Tonson; 4th, John Holmes; 5th, John, son of Roger Shackleton; 6th, Christopher Lupton; 7th, Richard Pighills.

"On August 20th, 1716, four of this town laid the four corner stones of the present school. Milo Gale, the Parson, that to the right in front. Mr. John Denbigh, a commission officer, that to the left at the south end. Mr. Richard Harper, that of the same end, to the west; and Mr. George Beanlands, that of the north end towards the west, being the present schoolmaster. Every one of which, depositing for the masons one shilling on his stone, wished prosperity to the building, and Timothy Rhoades, with his two men, proceeded in walling."

This school had been established previous to the death of the founder, as the following passage from Thoresby's Diary will prove. "Had good Mr. Gale's company about two hours. He shewed me a Free School, lately erected by Mr. John Drake, of Keighley, now living, who will settle the whole of his estate upon it at death." And we find, in Mr. Gale's list of the pew-holders in the Parish Church, 1703, that William Hanson held No. 2 for the school-house.

In compliance with Mr. Drake's wish, expressed in his will, the inhabitants of this parish, from the time of his death to the year 1841, continued to exempt the school property from all parochial taxes, "lays and impositions." When in that year, the Overseers supposing the estate liable, determined to have it taxed according to its valuation. But William Ellis, Esq. and Frederick Greenwood, Esq., the Magistrates, entertaining a doubt as to its liability, declined to issue a distress warrant against Mr. Thomas Wall, one of the tenants who refused to pay. In consequence, recourse was had to the Court of Queen's Bench, and a *rule nisi* was obtained in the Hilary Term, by Mr. Baines, for a *mandamus* to the defendants, calling upon them to levy upon Thomas Wall, the amount at which he had been assessed, and, on the 25th of November, 1842, Mr. Justice Wightman, in the absence of his learned friend, decided that the rule for the *mandamus* must be made absolute. Henceforward, in all probability, the estate will be required to bear its proper proportion of all parochial rates and assessments.

LIST OF SCHOOLMASTERS.

William Hanson was master in Mr. Drake's lifetime, but the first under the present foundation was George Beanlands, who died 1721, salary, £25, per annum. A vacancy here occurs of 35 years, but we are inclined to think that a Mr. Harrison preceded Leach. He supplied the church as Curate before the arrival of Mr. Knowlton, who, on the death of Mr. Pidding, had not completed his studies. He also officiated at Silsden Church.

Joseph Leach was appointed, 1757,—salary, £34. 10s.
Thomas Leeming succeeded Mr. Leach.
William Wilcock was appointed, 1773,—salary, £30.
William Hey ,, 1788, .. £40.
Christopher Atkinson ,, 1794, ,, £60.
Thomas Plummer ,, 1804, ,, £90.
Timothy Brayshaw, M.A., ,, 1840, ,, £100.

Alexander M'c Lean, B.A., succeeded Mr. Brayshaw who had resigned, 1846,—salary £120. per annum. The house and £10., with the writing and cyphering fees, were allowed towards the maintenance of an assistant.

The present Master, Mr. A. Crabtree, was appointed in 1854, at a stipend of £100 and school fees. His Assistant, Mons. Mercier, has about £50.

The Rev. Stephen Parkinson, M. A., Fellow and Tutor of St. John's College, Cambridge, and senior wrangler of his year, had his early education at this school.

TRUSTEES:—

William Busfeild, M.A., Rector.
John G. Sugden, Esq., Eastwood House, Keighley.
Frederick Greenwood, Esq., Norton Conyers.
Mr. Christopher Netherwood, London.
Mr. Benjamin F. Marriner, Spring Gardens, Keighley,
Mr. Joseph Smith, Beech Cliffe, Keighley.
Mr. John Bairstow, New Bridge-street, Keighley.

THE LOWER FREE SCHOOL.

The lower Free School, or, as it is sometimes called, the Usher School, was founded by Mr. Jonas Tonson, and first built at Exleyhead, on the site now occupied by the parish workhouse. But it appears at a vestry meeting, held June 30th, 1739, it was agreed to take the old school-house, at Exleyhead, for the use of the poor, at the yearly rent of forty shillings, which agreement, or resolution, was sanctioned by the names of the following parishioners:—

John Moorhouse.	John Sharpe.	David Brigg.
William Clapham.	John Roper.	Robert Sugden.
Joseph Wright.	John Binns.	James Greenwood.
Richard Pighells.	Richard Rawling.	Richard Moore.
	William Hartley.	William Paget.

The present school was built by subscription, with the approbation of Mr. Drake's trustees, on land adjoining the Free Grammar School. Though the original endowment was only £100., this sum appears to have been so far augmented as to produce, at the present time, about £40. a year. Mr. Tonson, who resided at Exleyhead and was called by Parson Gale "an old fanatical Presbyterian," was one of Mr. Drake's trustees who so obstinately opposed him, which may be deemed a sufficient reason for the Parson's neglecting to notice his charity. Mr. William Bell Sewell, Surgeon, Mr. Jonathan Anderton, and Mr. John Carter, are the present trustees, 1857, and Mr. William Plummer, Schoolmaster.

COURT OF REQUESTS AND COUNTY COURT.

The Act for establishing the Court of Requests was first passed in 1776, amended in 1779, again altered in 1793, and still further reformed in 1839. The undermentioned were the Commissioners for the parish of Keighley, in 1784.

"Rev. Charles Knowlton, Clerk, John Craven, Jonathan Wright, James Barwick, John Greenwood, Joseph Smith, John Sugden, Thomas Cure, Samuel Blakey, Michael Cousen, Abraham Smith, John Clapham, Rev. Samuel Philips, Thomas Cockshott, James Greenwood, John Driver, William Guyer, William Newsholme, Christopher Smith, Thomas Horsfall, John Horsfall, being twenty-one residents and inhabitants within the said parish of Keighley."

But, notwithstanding the various patchings, alterations, and reforms, the old Court of Requests was destined, in 1847, to give place to the present County Court, now held monthly in the Court House, North-street (built 1831). Its allotted district contains the parishes of Keighley and Bingley; the township of Haworth, in the parish of Bradford, with the several townships of Silsden, Sutton, and Steeton-cum-Eastburn, in the parish of Kildwick. J. J. Lonsdale, Esq. is Judge; Mr. Thomas Waterworth, Clerk; Mr. Maud Scott, Bailiff; and John and James Scott, assistants. The Court is now held for the recovery of debts and damages to the amount of £50.

PREVAILING CUSTOMS AND FORMER AMUSEMENTS.

The barbarous custom of bull-baiting was formerly very common in this place. An old friend of ours could (1846) still remember the bull-ring being affixed to a large stone on the Church-Green, or Market-place. A vulgar notion was entertained by the inhabitants that the flesh was not fit for use, unless the animal had been previously baited, or worried with dogs. Indeed, in former times, the bull-ring appears to have been as essential as the stocks, the ducking stool, or the pillory, which, in those halcyon days of lynch law, figured in every parish. The singular custom also prevailed of burning a candle during the whole of the time that any bull's flesh was exhibited for sale, whether by night or day. This town was also noted for the breed of a celebrated game-cock, called "The Keighley Grey;" but thanks to the schoolmaster, cock-fighting is no longer considered a genteel or fashionable amusement; and the heartless miscreant, who can find pleasure in torturing the animal creation, needs now only to be looked for amongst the most vicious and depraved. About 1630, "Drunken Barnaby," or, as he is called by Whitaker, the "Rhyming Vagrant," found at least some of our ancestors partaking with joyous hilarity of a more innocent and life invigorating exercise. He says

> "Thence to Keighley, where are mountains,
> Steepy, threat'ning; lively fountains;
> Rising hills and pleasant valleys;
> *Bon socias* and good fellows—
> Jovial, jocund, jolly bowlers,
> As if they were the world's controllers."

The Bowling Green was situated on the west side of and parallel with the Church-Green, now the site of New Bridge-street; and an old house by the Beck-side was called Bowl Alley. This species of amusement continued to be much in vogue in the early days of Mr. Knowlton, who is said to have frequently engaged in the diversion, and shared in the hearty laugh of the 'jolly bowlers.'

Football was another common diversion of the bull-baiting, cock-fighting times. If we are to believe the garrulous tales of some old people, this play was sometimes carried to a riotous and dangerous extent, township being arrayed against township and village against village. Much excitement and alarm were often created by the great set matches between the Town and Parish of Keighley. But this fierce and vulgar diversion (as it was called) does not appear to have been peculiar to the country districts, as the concluding sentence of a short paragraph in "Pepy's Diary" will testify:—"1664--5, January 2nd. The street full of footballs, it being a great frost;" and this, it must must be observed, was in one of the streets of London.

Knor and spell is a game of long standing and still popular, though it has now a strong competitor in the play of cricket. Most of the rude diversions of the athletic of both sexes have given place to more humanizing modes of recreation; as chess, galas, pic-nics, railway excursions, musical entertainments, &c.; and no insignificant number of all ages now luxuriate in books and newspapers—a source of pleasure formerly unknown to the masses.

ANCIENT CUSTOM OF TOLLING THE PASSING-BELL.

The absurd custom of tolling the passing-bell in the dead time of night, when death happened at that dread season, in order, as was supposed to clear the air of demons, and give the devout an opportunity of praying for the soul's safe departure, was only abolished some eighty or ninety years ago. A number of careless younkers after a night's carousal at the "Dog and Gun," along with one James Lee, a well-known chimney-sweep, who, on purpose to annoy the company as they supposed, would be acting the 'old soldier' by feigning himself dead drunk. But determined not to be outdone by the sweep, a wicked imp of the party proposed to go to Old David, the sexton, and order him to toll the passing-bell on the pretended sudden death of poor James Lee. This was no sooner proposed than done. Old David having been roused from his slumber, rubbed his eyes, took his lantern, and immediately ascended to the belfry. Whilst pulling away, perhaps half asleep, and dreaming on nothing but his fee, the sweep, who well knew what was going forward, went softly up the steps, put his sooty head into the room, and in a hollow tone of voice asked the sexton whom he was tolling for. The sexton who had hitherto been somewhat sceptical on the subject of ghosts, was now suddenly convinced. He let go the bell-rope, fell upon his knees, and for the first time in his life is said to have attempted in earnest to say his prayers. This impious and dangerous frolic so terrified Old David that nothing could ever after prevail upon him

"On the departure of a soul,
At dead of night the bell to toll."

PASSING BELL.

When William the Conqueror devastated Yorkshire and Durham by fire and sword, he issued a decree forbidding any Englishman, on pain of death, to burn a light in his dwelling after the bell had tolled the curfew, or cover-fire. Until this very year we kept up the memory of that tyrannical law, by tolling the curfew-bell at eight o'clock in the evening. Though the origin of the evening-bell is associated with unpleasant memories, yet its hoary age invests it with such a high degree of interest, that we hope our present churchwardens will revive and sustain it, and not suffer it to fall into desuetude.

The annexed inscription or device which was to be seen on the front of an old house, standing at the corner of Low-street and Cook-lane, prior to 1845, will be recognized by many of the inhabitants as an old and familiar acquaintance. This building was a part of the "Golden Fleece," or head inn, and was purchased at the sale of the Parker property in Keighley, by the agent of Lord George H. Cavendish, proprietor of the "Devonshire Arms," in order to do away with the rivalry which had previously existed between the two inns. It was erected, as shown by the initials and date, by Robert Parker, in the year 1697, whose prevailing taste and charitable disposition will be noticed under the head—Marley.

Olim, Parkinson,   R. P.   Nuper, Slater,
Hodie, Parker,   1697.   Cras, nescio.

This quaint motto may be thus translated:—Parkinson formerly, and Slater lately, lived here; Parker lives here to-day, but who will live here to-morrow I know not.

This device, though rare and curious, does not appear to have been original, as may be seen in the following passage from "Pepy's Diary," in the entry commencing November 10th, 1662. "By and by came in the great Mr. Swinfen, the Parliament man, who among other discourse of the rise and fall of families, told us of Bishop Bridgeman (father of Sir Orlando) who lately hath bought a seat, anciently of the Levers, and then the Ashtons, and so he hath in his great hall window (having repaired and beautified the house) caused four places to be left for coates of armes. In one he hath put the Levers, with this motto 'Olim.' In another, the Ashtons, with this, 'Heri.' In the next, his own, with this, 'Hodie.' In the fourth, nothing but this motto, 'Cras nescio cujus.'"

ANCIENT FAMILY OF KEIGHLEY.

WE shall now endeavour to communicate the few particulars we have been able to collect relating to the once famous family of Keighley, who took their name from the town, and were lords of the place for many centuries; but as the principal male branches have long since become extinct, and as we have no pedigree at hand, it would be vain to attempt anything like a full consecutive account of so ancient a family. Our only course will be to present our materials in the order of time, beginning with

Ralph, who, with his son Richard, "conveyed the church of Keighley to the prior and canons of Bolton," sometime in the latter part of the twelfth century.

We next find "a Richard, and Adam, and Peter de Kyghley," probably brothers and sons of the devout Ralph, witnesses to a charter granted by Robert de Lacy, who died 1193; and in the Glusburn and Elslack papers, mentioned in the "Collectanea Topographica Geneologica," we find a Roger de Kytheley prior to the year 1243, and an Elias de Kighley previous to 1270.*

Probably the next in point of time will be Henry de Kygheley, one of the most conspicuous members of the family. He is said to have been the confidential servant of Henry, commonly called the great Earl of Lincoln, and held the offices of Steward and Master Forester of Balckburnshire, under that nobleman from 1288 to 1294, residing partly at Inskip and partly at Keighley. According to the manuscript pedigree recently discovered, he married "Ellen, daughter of Hugh Venables, Knight," and as stated in "Baines's History of Lancashire," thrice represented that county in parliament. "As the name of Keighley occurs amongst those Yorkshire knights, who served with King Edward the First in Scotland and elsewhere," it may be assumed, notwithstanding his eminence as a civilian and man of business, this Sir Henry, as he is styled in the pedigree, was likewise a soldier. Be this as it may, it was that 'great captain of the age' who conferred upon him the charter for a Market, Fair, and Free Warren, "which was accounted a very considerable favour in those days." It was probably not until the death of his old master, the Earl of Lincoln, that Henry Keighley, with one or

---

* A Gilbert de Kiggellay gave land to the priory of Selby, about 1260. We can only account for the various ways of spelling Keighley by supposing the ear to have often guided the pen.

two of his refractory neighbours, received from Edward II. the royal injunction and command to become the proper homagers and vassals of Robert, the first Lord Clifford, of the barony of Skipton. "He held lands in Keighley, Utley, &c.;" and Camden, speaking of him in 1607, says he was "interred here."

Richard de Kyghley, as we find in Whitaker's "History of Craven," was lord of the manor of Keighley, 1316. He had probably a son and heir of the same name, besides younger sons, from one of which the well-known personage described as Gilbert Keighley of Utley, derived.

He had likewise a daughter "Alice, who married Richard Dyneley of Downham, in Lancashire."

The following from the Ffarynton Pedigree proves that the above Henry had a daughter Clarissa, and that the family had obtained possession of, and sometimes resided at, Inskip, in the parish of St. Michael's le Wire, about the commencement of the fourteenth century.

"William de Ffaryngton, to whom was granted 22nd of Edward III., 1349, a right of Park and Free Warren, in Leyland and Farmiston, was the eldest son of Sir John Ffaryngton, by Clarissa, daughter of ———— de Keighley, of Inskip."

The succeeding article, transcribed from the account book of the Comptroller of the Wardrobe of Edward II., and brought to light by the Record Commission, affords an interesting glance at the period to which it refers.

"To Ralph de Arynburgh and Roger de Kygheley, slingers, coming from the garrison of Berwick to the King for relief, and sent to religious houses in order to have sustenance there during the rest of their lives," &c. The abbeys and priories in those disorderly times were obliged to maintain a certain number of soldiers, chiefly the younger sons of gentlemen, in order to defend them against the Scots, and other bands of ruffians, their own countrymen, who subsisted entirely upon plunder. This Roger de Kygheley may have been a younger brother of Henry, who represented the county of Lancaster in parliament.

William de Kygheley was witness to a deed at Skipton in the year 1331, or fourth of Edward III.; and a Nicholas Kygheley we find mentioned in the Glusburn and Elslack charter, 1373.

Presuming we have now arrived at the proper time for introducing the names of Gilbert and Margaret, the date of whose monuments have been the subject of considerable misapprehension; and believing, from the agreement in the names and other circumstances, the following somewhat disjointed fragments to have reference to them, we venture to place the date of their sepulture in the latter part of the fourteenth century, and from the symbolical evidence on the husband's monument, conjecture that he was some noted but unlucky soldier actively engaged in the latter part of the troublesome and unfortunate reign of Richard II.

In the pedigree of the family of Leeds in Thoresby's History, it is stated that Margery, daughter of ———— Hornby, who had been previously married to Sir Robert Urswick, and afterwards to Sir Gilbert Kyghley, was again married to Alexander de Leeds. We are also informed in Baines's "History of Lancashire" that in the year 1380, the Duke of Lancaster, issued a mandate commanding John Radcliffe to seize the land of Gilbert de Kygheley and others. What may have been the cause of this seizure and confiscation we know not, but find that the manor of Utley, of which Gilbert Keighley was probably lord, had escheated to the Crown, and was in course of time granted by King Henry VIII. to John Carr, Knight. It is likewise recorded in another part of the last-named work, that in the year 1384, the Duke of Lancaster granted to Richard de Houghton, who appointed William de Hornby, parson of St. Michael's upon Wyre, the enrolment of the wardship of lands of Henry de Kighley, Knight, in Lancashire and Yorkshire, and the marriage of his son. How nearly the deceased knight was related to the above Gilbert and Margaret we know not, but we suppose that the ties of consanguinity alone may have entitled Parson Hornby to a right to that important place of trust.

Since the foregoing particulars were put down a pedigree of this ancient family has been discovered in the library of the British Museum by Mr. Busfeild, a neighbouring antiquary, a portion of which we here subjoin. "This Henry was succeeded by Sir Gilbert Keighley, whose monumental stone has been described. Sir Gilbert's son and successor was Richard Keighley, living in the 20th of Edward III. (1347), and who paid aid for making the King's eldest son a knight. He had issue William, living about the 36th of Edward III., whose son and heir Henry, married Margaret, daughter of Sir Robert Hesketh, Knight."

Without venturing an opinion as to the correctness of the passage here cited, we pass on to the following account given in a note attached to the Pedigree:—
" Sir Gilbert is buried in the north quire of the church, under a stone inscribed '*Gilbertus Kyghley de*

Utlay, miles jacet hic tumulatus,' &c., which I see in June, 1667." What then becomes of the absurd date, 1022? The writer here quoted would have been a strange person indeed if, after having convinced himself of the correctness of this date, he had, contrary to his convictions, and in order to fill up a gap in the Pedigree, thought proper to place the knight and his lady once more on the stage of life after a long sleep of more than three hundred years. From what is here stated the original reading of the inscription on the stone must have run thus;—*Gilbertus Kyghley de Utlay, miles, jacet hic tumulatus, et Margaria uxores, A. O. Dm.*, (Date uncertain, but doubtless in the fourteenth century.)

Adam de Keighley was summoned as one of twelve jurors by William de Nessfield, who was Seneschal under John of Gaunt, Duke of Lancaster, 1390. Richard de Kyghley, mentioned in the compotas of Bolton, 4th of Henry V., married the daughter of Walter Calverley of Calverley, and was living about 1445.

Dr. Whitaker says of the ancient family of this name, "I have met with the following memorials during the age of chivalry, in the 6th of Henry VI. Sir John de Kighley, Knight, accompanied Humphrey, Duke of Gloucester, to recover the town and castle of Crotoye, in France, with thirty men at arms, of which himself and one other were knights, the rest esquires, and ninety archers. In the eighth of the same reign he was once more retained to serve beyond the sea, with twenty-nine men at arms besides himself."

"Sir Henry Kighley, Knight, attended Robert Lord Willoughby de Broke, with 380 soldgurs, to Bretagne, 4th of Henry VII."

This aged warrior appears also to have taken a

conspicuous part in the battle of Flodden Field; for it is stated in Ridpath's "Border History," that, "On the other side of the field, Sir William Stanley, by the incessant shot of archers commanded by himself, Sir William Molyneux, Sir Henry Kighley, and others from Lancashire and Cheshire, forced the Scots to break their array and come down to more even ground, where, being attacked by three different bands, they were discomfited and put to flight; the Earls of Argyle and Lennox being slain on the spot." The annexed lines will prove the historical correctness of the Scottish bard.

> "Charge, Chester, charge! on, Stanley, on!
> Were the last words of Marmion."

Richard Keighley, whose daughter married William Gascoigne of Lasingcroft, was one of the feoffees in trust for Sir Robert Plumpton, 1501, and also, with many others, witness to an award at the Chapel on the Bridge in York, in a dispute between Sir Richard Plumpton and Sir Richard Empson, Knight, 20th Henry VII.

In Watson's "History of the House of Warren" we are informed that George Kighley, Esq., born about 1506, married Anne Warren, and had by her Henry, who married, 1561, the daughter of Sir Alexander Osbaldiston of Osbaldiston Hall, Lancashire, and had Catharine and Anne; Catharine marrying Thomas Worsley of Booths; and Anne, Sir William Cavendish of Hardwick, then Baron Cavendish of Hardwick. The lady who carried the manor and estates at Keighley to the noble house of Cavendish, is said by Whitaker to have been "interred under a splendid monument at Haut Hacknall, near Hardwick, in Derbyshire."

This ancient House bore argent a fess, sable: crest, a dragon's head, couped, sable.

An offshoot appears to have flourished for a short time in west Derby, as we find it stated in "Burke's Peerage" that, "Thomas Houghton, Esq., of Houghton Tower, who served the office of Sheriff of Lancashire in the sixth year of the reign of Queen Elizabeth, and fell in a duel with the Baron of Walton, had married Anne, daughter of Henry Kighley, Esq., son and heir of Sir Henry Kighley, Knight, by whom he had several children." We also collect from Baines's "History of Lancashire," that in a muster-roll of soldiers for the county of Lancaster, Anno 1574, Ellis Kighley, for West Derby hundred, was to furnish one coat-plate, one pyke, one black-bill, and one marriane; in the same year for the hundred of Amounderness, Henry Kighley to furnish one coat-plate, one longbow, one sheaf of arrows, and one scull-bill. We also find Elizabeth Kighley, a popish recusant, mentioned 1573.

As a proof of the high estimation in which the family was held, we may observe (though the statement cannot be reconciled with Mr. Watson's account) that the important families of Preston, of Holker Hall, and Hulton of Hulton Park, considered it no disparagement to claim a family connection or alliance with them; as on a reference to their respective pedigrees in John Burke's "History of the Landed Gentry" may be seen. "Catharine, daughter of Sir Thomas Preston, Knight, of Preston Hall, and Levins, in Westmoreland, and of Furnace Abbey, and Holkar Hall, Lancashire, married Sir Thomas Carus,

Knight, one of the Judges of the Court of King's Bench in the time of Elizabeth, and had, with other issue, Mary Carus, who wedded Henry Kighley, Esq., of Kighley, in Yorkshire, and had a daughter, Anne Kighley, who espoused Sir William Cavendish, and from this marriage the late Duke of Devonshire derives." To which is added the following note:— "Lord George Augustus Henry Cavendish, now Earl of Burlington, inherits from his uncle, the late Lord George Cavendish, the devisee of Sir William Lowther, Holker Park and other great estates in Lancashire, formerly belonging to the Preston Family."

Another considerable branch which may be supposed from the addition of the mullet to derive from the third son of Ralph, was settled at New Hall, near Otley, and was allied by marriage to many of the chief families in the neighbourhood. They had also possessions in Cleveland in this county, where they sometimes resided.

In the "Plumpton Correspondence" published by the Camden Society, we find a Lawrence Kighley, mentioned as one of the trustees in a Deed of Settlement for the Plumpton family, bearing date 1464. He was afterwards chosen, along with Robert Roos, of Ingmanthorpe as arbitrator on the part of Sir William Plumpton, in a dispute between that gentleman and the minister and canons of the house of St. Robert, near Knaresborough, 1471.

Thomas Kighley of New Hall, living 1505, married Dorothy, daughter of John Vavasour of Weston. Alice Kighley of New Hall married —— Kaye of Woodsome, in the parish of Almondbury, whose arms are still to be seen there in an old family picture.

In the "Plumpton Correspondence" we also find

that another Lawrence Kighley of New Hall married Isabel, daughter of Ralph, Lord Neville, son and heir apparent of Ralph, Earl of Westmoreland, and by indenture made March 10th, 1528—9, between William Plumpton, Esq., of one party: "The lands, &c., lying in Roughfarlington, in the county of York, except the New House and the Orchard, together with other premises in Plumpton and Knaresborough, assigned to Dame Isabel Plumpton, late wife of Sir Robert Plumpton, Knight, and now wife of the said Lawrence, in the name of her feofment, were exchanged for a rent-charge of twenty marks annually during the joint lives of the said Lawrence and Isabel, and if the said Lawrence fortune to die, leaving the said Isabel, she to enter upon and have the same during her natural life." Dame Isabel Plumpton was second wife of Lawrence Kighley; his first wife was Anne, daughter of Thomas Lyndley of Scuttershelf-cum-Ebor, Esq. The daughter of the above Lawrence married Robert Dyneley of Bramhope, of the house of Downham, about 1550.

Edmund, or Edward Kighley of Newhall married Anne, daughter and sole heiress of William Goldesbury of Goldesbury, and had issue Leonard Kighley, who sold the Newhall property to Mr. Proctor, a gentleman of the law, about the year 1589.

In addition to the above, we find in Graves's "History of Cleveland," that John Kighley was Rector of Kildale, North Riding, 1436, Patron, John de Percy. He was afterwards presented to the Rectory of Kilderwell by Thomas Lumley. The same historian also informs us that "Lawrence Kighley married Anne Lindley of Skuttershelf, and that they had a son Thomas, and Thomas had a son Lawrence, who sold the third part of Skuttershelf to Thomas Layton, his cousin."

Now, fortunately, this Thomas Layton turns out to be the connecting link between the Newall and senior branch, as the reader will probably remember we were told by Mr. Gale that a free-rent of £3. 2s. per annum was paid out of the mill at Keighley to Thomas Layton of Rawden; it being quite evident that the Laytons became entitled to this free-rent in consequence of their connection with the Kighleys of Newall.

This branch of the family bore argent, on a fess, sable, a mullet, or, the mullet for difference.

NOBLE FAMILY OF CAVENDISH.

From the death of Henry Kighley in the latter part of Elizabeth, the valuable possessions in this parish descended through the Dukes of Devonshire to the late Lord George Cavendish, uncle to His Grace the present Duke, and who in 1831 was created by William IV. Earl of Burlington and Baron Cavendish of Keighley. "Lord George was grandson of the late Earl of Burlington, that eminent nobleman so celebrated for his taste in Architecture, who died in 1735, after the title which was first conferred on his grandfather, Richard second Earl of Cork, in 1664, had existed about 70 years." William, the second Earl of the noble House of Cavendish, was the first to assume as his grandfather's heir apparent, the title of Baron Cavendish of Kighley. It is a circumstance worthy of remark that the advowson of this church, which was severed from the manor and estate by Ralph Keighley in the twelfth century should, after the lapse of six hundred years, again revert to his lineal descendant, who now retains the patronage of the living. This singular restoration was effected in the following manner:—

"The priory of Bolton was dissolved the 11th of June, 1540, and in 1543 was granted to Henry Clifford, Earl of Cumberland, in which family it was retained to 1635, when Elizabeth, the daughter and sole heiress of Henry the last Earl of Cumberland marrying Richard the first Earl of Burlington, carried the demesnes into the family, whose daughter Charlotte, sole heiress, married in 1748 the Duke of Devonshire." Thus the right of presentation which had been alienated by the pious and devout Ralph, was in the course of revolving years again restored to the hands of his illustrious descendant. But owing to the long life of Mr. Knowlton, William Spencer, the present Duke, was the first Cavendish who had an opportunity of presenting to the living, and Theodore Dury, M. A., the first presentee.

The shield borne by the Keighleys of Keighley and Inskip, delineated in the title page, was formerly to be seen in the lower portion of the north-west angle of the old steeple. It is also noticed in Berry's Heraldic Dictionary, and will probably be hereafter adopted as the arms of the town. By some mistake in the confusion of re-building, that shield was replaced by the arms of the Keighleys of Newhall, a younger branch of the same family, as may be observed on the front of the present steeple, between the symbols of Messrs. Dury and Busfeild, late and present Rectors.

ROMAN ROADS AND COINS.

The Roman conquerors of Britain, having subdued the country and securely stationed their legions, seeing they only possessed the beak and talons of the eagle without its wings, began without delay, like prudent settlers, to construct their military-ways and intermediate outposts between one station or colony and another, detached fragments of which are still to be seen in many places, whilst portions of others lying in or about the cultivated ground, visible at a comparatively recent period, are now only to be traced in the pages of the historian.

The road from Manchester to Ilkley, "After passing Blackstone-edge, leaving Halifax considerably on the right and Illingworth a little on the left, the line passes through Denholme Park, and runs to the west of Cullingworth, and between Cullingworth and Hainworth it is visible as a paved way more than twelve feet broad, and neatly set with stones of the country. It is found in several places upon Harden Moor, crossing the heights of the common, and pointing on the Moorhouse above Morton, and it is again visible on Rumbles Moor. Upon this wild heath it appears, as I am informed a raised, paved road overgrown with turf, keeping upon the shelves of the hills, to avoid the cliffs on oue side and the morasses on the other, pointing directly to the valley of the Wharfe, and the village of Ilkley within it."*

After many a fruitless ramble on Harden Moor in

---

* Mr. Whitaker's "History of Manchester."

search of this road, we were at length shown a small portion of it near to a farm-house called Kesty or Casty Wood, and to our great delight we have since seen more than one hundred yards of it dug up in an allotment on the moor, near Shay-delf, belonging to Mr. John Spencer, Hainworth; and we were curious enough to remove the thin turf from a part and sweep it for more minute inspection. The stones, apparently hardly touched by the hammer, lie, as might be expected, with an uneven surface in many places, and are of various sizes, but mostly small, the larger laid flat and the smaller edgeways, and not well adapted for ease of foot to the traveller. At the south-east corner of the above allotment two paths cross over an exposed part of this interesting relic of Roman industry. But the road from Manchester to Ilkley was crossed at this place by another, a portion of which has been long known to the writer. It was, previous to the opening of a stone quarry in its neighbourhood, strikingly plain and complete. One end of it is connected with the old road to Halifax, whilst the other is lost upon the common, but appearing again, as we are told, in the neighbourhood of Hewnden, and pointing in the direction of Slack, in the parish of Huddersfield, the Cambodunum of the Romans, from some place in the north-west. We are informed by the competent authority before cited, that "The only determinate characteristic of a station is either the appellation of *caster* affixed to the place, or the concurrence of Roman roads at the point. This," as he observes, "has never yet been sufficiently attended to by the antiquarian critic, and for want of such a decisive standard, the mind has been left to brood fondly over its own unguarded ideas, and to multiply stations at the random suggestions of the fancy."

We shall perhaps be justified, according to the rule laid down, in claiming for 'Casty Wood' the rank of one of those small stations or military outposts, so necessary in a country kept under subjection by a foreign power, for the various purposes of exploration, for affording shelter and accommodation to travellers, protection to convoys, and procuring provisions for the camp. We are the more strongly inclined to this opinion from the fact, that many years ago, as some labourers were searching for coal in a field near the farm-house, they were surprised to meet with a number of bricks several feet below the surface, and were at a loss to account for their appearance in that place. There were many such out-posts, as we are informed, in the neighbourhood of Manchester, and on the military ways leading from thence to the more important stations.

The Roman road from Ilkley to Ribchester, another well-known station, probably crossed the stream of the Aire at Longlands-ford, and wound under the hill to Steeton; from which place it appears to have proceeded by two separate branches, one through Aiden to Colne, the Roman Colonio, and thence to Ribchester; the other in nearly a direct line from Steeton through Gisburn to Lancaster. The word Aiden is said by Camden to signify a station for a small party of horse; and Steeton, which in ancient deeds is designated Stiveton, if not a personal appellation answering to Stephen, is probably a corruption of Street-town. There is a line of road at this place still known by the name of Wood-street.

The following account by Dr. Whitaker, of the

great Discovery of Roman coins at Elam Grange, will be found appended to Thoresby's Catalogue of Antiquities in the "History of Leeds:"—" The next is perhaps the noblest discovery ever made in Roman Britain. March 7th, 1775, as a farmer was making a drain in a field at Morton Banks, near Bingley, he struck upon the remains of a copper chest about twenty inches beneath the surface, which contained nearly 100 lbs. weight of Roman denarii. There was also in the chest a silver image (I have not heard of what deity) about six inches long. They included every Emperor from Nero to Pupienus, Pertinax and Didius Julianus only excepted, together with many Empresses, and a variety of reverses."

This treasure, supposed to have been a military chest buried near to a line of road on some sudden emergency, was found by Simon Mitchell. Elam Grange is nearly opposite to Utley, and not far from Longlands-ford, the part of the stream already pointed out as the most likely to have been forded by the Roman legions.

CELTS, URNS, AND OTHER ANTIQUITIES.

A NUMBER of copper celts was found a few years ago at Brunthwaite-crag, and sold, we believe, to Mr. J. Laycock for old metal, but we trust that some of them are still carefully preserved; and whilst excavating for the Railway within about a hundred yards of the Keighley station, one of the labourers discovered three urns containing a quantity of human bones. Two of them were unluckily broken, one being large enough to hold eight or nine quarts. The one brought away whole, and seen by the present writer, may hold about a quart; it is somewhat tastefully designed, moulded by hand out of common clay, without glaze, and rudely ornamented on the outside by some sharp instrument. The once animated contents of each urn were covered by a square flat stone. Part of a quern or hand-mill was likewise found in cutting this part of the line, which is now in the possession of Mr. Wm. Lund.

On Harden Moor, about two miles south of Keighley, we meet with an interesting plot of ground where was to be seen in the early days of many aged persons yet living, a cairn or 'skirt of stones,'* which appears to have given name to the place, now designated Cat or Scat-stones. This was no doubt the grave of some noted but long-forgotten warrior.

Cairns are composed of stones of all dimensions thrown together in a conical form, a flat stone crowning the apex. In general, these accumulations appear to have been designed for the sepulchral protection of heroes and great men. Stone chests, the repository of urns and ashes, are lodged in the earth beneath; sometimes only one, sometimes more, are found thus deposited, and Mr. Pennant mentions an instance of seventeen being discovered under the same pile. They may justly be supposed to have been proportioned in size to the rank of the person, or to his popularity; the people of whole districts assembled to shew their respect to the deceased, and by an active honouring of his memory, soon accumulated heaps equal to those which astonish us at this time. But these honours were not merely those of the day; as long as the

---

* The Cairn was called Skirtstones by the country people in allusion to the custom of carrying a stone in the skirt to add to the Cairn.

ANTIQUITIES.

memory of the deceased endured, seldom a passenger went by without adding a stone to the heap; for the neglect of which they were supposed to be visited by some terrible calamity.

The fine piece of ground called 'Cat-stones,' is enclosed on three sides by a considerable bank of earth, and bears evident marks of the plough. The country people believe it to have been an intrenchment or camp. Opposite to this place, and near to Flappet-springs, there remains about one-fourth part of a considerable rampart, the portion of a circle about eighty yards in diameter; the height of the embankment above the internal area varies from two to four feet, and from the bottom of the external ditch, three to seven feet; it is at present, 1857, crowned with a beautiful dwarf furze. Half of this earth-work is distinctly traceable; but the tasteless, demolishing spirit of the age, will, it is feared, soon obliterate the last vestige of this connecting link between ancient and modern days. It is known in the neighbourhood by the name of 'Castlestead-ring.' Respecting this place, Mr. James, in his "History of Bradford," observes that "if not intended for the folding or shelter of cattle and called 'Cattlestead-ring,' it may have been one of a line of forts raised by the Lancashire and Yorkshire Britons in their wars upon each other." But may it not have been a less permanent camp thrown up by the Danes in one of their sudden incursions into the south-western parts, and its original name not 'Castle,' but 'Campstead-ring'? Similar rings of different proportions exist in other parts of Yorkshire. At Tanfield, on the river Ure, are three circular intrenchments about half a mile asunder and in a right line.

DISSENTING PLACES OF WORSHIP.

INDEPENDENTS.

From the commencement of the civil wars in 1642 to the Restoration in 1660, the political bias of religious parties in Keighley appears to have been anti-monarchical; and it will be observed that whether the national saddle was mounted by Episcopalian, Presbyterian, or Independent, Rector Claver, true to his conscience like the Vicar of Bray, still kept possession of his benefice. He appears to have died a few months after the Restoration.

In consequence, as we are informed, of the severity of the then existing laws against dissenters from the national worship, few chapels had been erected previous to 1672, such places being denounced as conventicles for illegal assemblies, and the worshippers therein subjected to every species of annoyance. But Charles the Second, in order, as alleged by some historians, to afford relief to the Roman Catholics, found it expedient in that year to abrogate or suspend the penal statutes against dissenters. Yet it was not until the Revolution in 1688 that our legislators began to perceive the impossibility of forcing conviction or controlling thought. In the time of Mr. Gale, who died, 1721, there appears to have been only one dissenting place of worship in this town, and that was occupied by the Society of Friends; and although in his account of the establishment of the Grammar School, he assigns the lack of knowledge as the reason why some of his parishioners had been led astray by a party of persons whom he designated Anabaptists, yet it is quite certain that he must have misapplied that word or purposely used it as a term of reproach for the Presbyterians, as the Anabaptists, properly so called, had no society here before the year 1809, nor had they any in the neighbouring towns till long after Mr. Gale's time. That there was no Presbyterian place of worship may be readily inferred, for in his quarrel with Robert Hall of Newsholme and Jonas Tonson of Exleyhead, two of the trustees of the Free School, he says, in reference to the latter gentleman, "I told Mr. Isaac Hollings that he was a fanatical Presbyterian, running after the schismatical worship of Bingley Chapel, and therefore envied anything done for the Church." The Presbyterian Chapel at Bingley, as we observe in Oliver Heywood's Diary, had been erected previous to 1673, and probably served for a considerable district. Fortunately for our purpose, Mr. R. Atkinson, Exleyhead, has shown us some MS. verses, composed by his great-grandfather, Wm. Clapham, a member of Keighley Church during the incumbency of the Rev. Mr. Collins, wherein he laments a defection from the Church which then occurred, and caused, as he says, by the weak voice and defective articulation of Mr. Collins, and his refusal to comply with the entreaties of his flock to employ a curate. These dissidents, in concert with the Presbyterians who had previously attended Bingley Chapel, began to worship in a laith belonging to one Leach. As the Rev. Messrs. Wickham and Collins divide the period, 1721—1736 between them, and Mr. Collins succeeded Mr. Wickham and as the secession would probably happen soon after Mr. Collins's appointment, we may fix the date about the year 1730. The new society was essentially Presbyterian, and its early ministers were of that persuasion, but some time prior to 1770, it had merged into Independency. Mr. Niel, a talented Scotch student, prematurely yielding to the impulsive force of love and conjugal affection against the laws of the Kirk, was dismissed by his inexorable presbytery; and notwithstanding the ban of the Kirk, was invited by the society of Keighley to become their pastor. He was ordained according to the Independent form in 1756, and settled here until 1770, during which time it is probable the society would become thoroughly Independent. Their first humble meeting-house fell down one Sunday-night just after the small congregation had left it. A little chapel was then built, which gave place to another in 1820, and this, in its turn, was superseded by the present beautiful chapel, which was opened in 1856. Its style is Italian, cost £4000., with 1000 sittings. During the twenty-three years' pastorate of the present minister, the Rev. J. Tattersfield, the members have increased nearly four-fold.

SOCIETY OF FRIENDS.

As faithful chroniclers of the past we must lift the veil from the shady side of the ecclesiastical portion of our narrative. Every christian reader of history has often to lament over the strange association of contradictory practices exhibited in the lives of men distinguished alike for piety to God and a desire to promote the best interests of their fellow-creatures. The holy apostles, James and John, in their warm displeasure against the Samaritans, said, "Lord, wilt thou that we command fire to come down from heaven, and consume them, even as Elias did." The human heart is still the same, and our Saviour's rebuke to his infatuated disciples, "ye know not what manner of spirit ye are of," is equally applicable to us. We were forcibly impressed with this humbling truth while recently perusing Bartlett's "Pilgrim Fathers." These pious men, who were persecuted for conscience' sake, fled to the Continent, and afterwards to America. Soon after establishing themselves there, a few of their community embraced the doctrines of the Friends; and, "tell it not in Gath, publish it not in the streets of Askelon," lest the enemy rejoice, these very men who had themselves suffered the loss of all things for conscience' sake, imprisoned the innocent converts, and persecuted them even unto death! The same spirit has actuated every dominant party in every age and country. There is, however, a difference in degree; for, as in the days of St. Paul, the strictest sect has ever been the least tolerant. It is well for this country that the broad catholic principles of our venerable establishment, freed from the bane of compulsory appliance, permit every man to worship God under his own vine and under his own fig-tree.

Most of our old churches were built and endowed by the wealthy for the joint benefit of themselves and their neighbours. A part of the endowment generally consisted of a share of the yearly produce of all or a portion of the donor's lands. In the eventful course of time many of these lands passed into different families, and some of those families left the Establishment and joined the denominations which sprang up in the reign of Queen Elizabeth; and, as might be expected, their respect for the Establishment which they had left decreased in proportion as their affection increased for the denomination which they had joined. This loss of respect for the mother-church soon blinded the eyes of many to a sense of what was right and just, and they refused to pay to the clergyman his share of the yearly produce of the properties which they held on the very condition that the said yearly produce should be duly rendered. Hence, when an incumbent had occasion to seek the aid of the magistrate to obtain his temporal rights, a cry broke forth of persecution for conscience' sake. We feel sure the candid reader, who has maturely considered this subject, will agree with us in deploring the inconsistency and injustice of those parties who attempt to shuffle off a duty and a claim on the false plea of conscience' sake, and who at the same time profess to believe that it is better to obey than to sacrifice. With these views we cannot but deem the conduct of those persons mentioned in our quotations as refusing to pay tithe of corn to be entirely unjustifiable.*

We yield to none in our abhorrence of the Act of Uniformity and all similar measures; they are dark spots in our annals — beacons to warn us against occupying the seat of the Judge of all the earth. They remind us of the monk-emperor of Germany, Charles the Fifth, who having made a number of clocks, and having long tried in vain to make them keep time together, exclaimed, "What a fool I am, I have all my life been trying to make all my subjects think alike, and I cannot make even a few clocks go alike!" It is no wonder then that when the civil powers armed our former rectors with authority to inflict

---

* The only valid objection against paying the *full tithe* of corn, &c., is where the land has been improved by the objector.

fines for non-attendance at the parish church, or worshipping at other places, or not tendering the dues founded on ancient usage, we find them occasionally repeating the vain attempts of the monk-emperor and mulcting refractory parishioners. We should rather wonder that the instances are so few, and regard them as a proof that our rectors must have been upon the whole very kind and gentle shepherds.

The Society of Friends was established here in the days of the Commonwealth, and within a few years of the origin of the sect. The following particulars are extracted from a manuscript formerly belonging to this religious community in Keighley, containing a register of baptisms, marriages and deaths, commencing with the year 1654 and ending about 1760, with an account of the sufferings they endured. This register contains 148 births, 48 marriages and 171 deaths.

"Jonas Smith of Stanbury, for tythe of wool and lambs demanded by Timothy Middleton, impropriator, and for not giving an answer into the Exchequer upon oath, was imprisoned in Pontefract Low Jail from the first day of the twelfth month, 1655, unto the twenty-second of the sixth month, 1656."

"Taken from William Clough of Keighley, by Thomas Danby, Priest of Keighley, or his agents, tythe-corn and hay to the value of £1. 4s. Taken from Thomas Taylor of Laycock, for the same Priest, one horse worth £3. for tythe and Easter-offerings, which the said T. Taylor for conscience' sake could not pay."

"Thomas Brigg, senior, in the parish of Keighley, for denying to pay tythe-corn, had taken from him by Thomas Danby, the Priest, pewter to the value of £1. 10s."

"Same person for steeple-house assessment, by Richard Shackleton, John Clerk, Walter Butler and Francis Widdop, pewter worth £1. 10s., 1662."

"Robert Hudson of Keighley, for tythe, 9s.; and moreover because the said Robert Hudson could not in conscience' sake answer the priest's will in paying him his demands for tythes, &c., the said priest, namely Thomas Danby, prosecuted the said Robert Hudson in the Upper Bench to an Outlawry, unknown to the said R. Hudson, and thereupon cast him into York Jail, and was continued prisoner upon this account for six years and ten months, 1666."

"Taken from T. Brigg, senior, tythe-corn for three years, £1. 10s. by the Priest of Keighley, 1679."

"Thomas Pearson of Keighley, for absenting from the National Worship, and for not appearing to a citation issued out of the Ecclesiastical Court, was prosecuted to an *Excommunica Capiendo*, and committed to prison at York Jail, the 15th day of the first month, 1679, and remained several years."

"Thomas Taylor, Thomas Brigg, junior, William Smith, and Jo. Hird, being apprehended by the constable of Keighley upon a capital warrant, were conveyed to the sessions at Gisburn, the 29th day of the first month, 1682, and being brought before the Magistrates, they were required to give bond and find surety for their good behaviour, and to appear at the sessions at Wetherby. Which thing they were not free to do, forasmuch as they were not conscious of any ill behaviour. Therefore they were committed by Jo. Ashton, Henry Marsden, Thomas Parker, Christopher Wilkinson, and Thomas Heber, Justices so called, to the Castle of York, and they continued prisoned on the account near four months, and they were released at the general sessions at Pontefract."

"Richard Shackleton of Harden, being at a meeting of the people called Quakers, at Stubbing House, and being fined on the account of some that did bear a public testimony for the truth, because of the poverty of the said friend or friends, that did declare to the value of £11., by order of the Lord Fairfax, so called, Thomas Fairfax, and Walter Calverley, called Justices, and some goods upon agreement by some of his relations unknown to him were returned again. However, he suffered, notwithstanding what was returned again, to the value of £10. 5s."

"In the year 1660 a number of Friends being met together to wait upon God in a peaceable and christian manner, at Laycock, near Keighley, the constable of Keighley sent a company of rude men with club, bill, and staves, who did violently pull Joseph Jescop and William Clayton out of the meeting, with twenty more, and carried them before Charles Fairfax of Menston, called a Justice, who tendered them the oath of allegiance which for conscience' sake and in obedience to the commands of Christ they would not take, and so they were committed by him to the Castle of York, where they remained six weeks and were then released by the Judge."

"Alvery Baraclough, Thomas Taylor, J. Brooksbank, and Robert Smith, being of the number of those last mentioned who were sent to jail, had goods taken from them by Jo. Denbigh, constable of Keighley, to the value of £1. 4s. for carrying them to jail."

"Friends being met peaceably to worship God at Steeton, there came in two rude men with a sword and a staff, and pulled William Smith, Jo. Smith, John Brooksbank, and T. Taylor, with some others, out of the house, and carried them to Skipton, where they were closely confined for about two days without any bedding, and were had before Colonel Pudsey and Cuthbert Wade, Justices, so called, who committed them to York Castle for denying to swear, where they remained three weeks, and were released by the Duke of Buckingham."

"Adam Bell, Abraham Bell, John Drake, senior, John Drake, his son, Jonas Bottomley, Richard Shackleton, John Milner and John Eastburn were all taken by Capias Warrant and brought to the Sessions at Wakefield, and refusing to swear, were all committed prisoners to York Castle, by Jo. Kay, Jo. Peebles and Jasper Blytheman, and remained there three years and eight months, when they were released by virtue of a warrant given forth at Whitehall by King James the Second, on the fifteenth day of the first month, 1686."

"Miles Gale, Priest of Keighley, summoned the following persons for church-dues in the Court belonging to the manor of Keighley, whereupon John Stones, Bailiff of the said Court, by warrant, and Thomas Stones, his son, and Thomas Dickinson, his assistant, came the seventh day of the twelfth month, 1698, and made distress as follows, viz.:—Thomas Brigg, goods to the value of £1. 4s.; John Hird, £2. 15s.; James Ramsden, £1. 4s.; John Smith and William Smith, £2. 4s."

"Miles Gale, Priest of Keighley, having put the late act in force, the Friends were summoned before Henry Currer and Robert Ferrand, Justices of Peace. The priest's demand was for five years past, but the Justices could only allow for two years by the same statute; and Daniel Green and Abraham Beanlands,

SOCIETY OF FRIENDS.

two of the Churchwardens, brought them again before the Justices after they were departed, to shew cause why they refused to pay the steeple-house tax, and the Justices granted warrant to Daniel Green, John Drake, William Beanlands, William Clark, Churchwardens, and they were fined as follows (1704):— Taken from Thomas Brigg, Calversyke-hill, bacon, wheat and barley worth £1. 5s. 4d.; Richard Waddington, bacon, £1. 13s. 8d."

"Miles Gale, Priest of Keighley, made complaint before William Busfield and Robert Ferrand, Justices of the Peace, who granted their warrant to Lawrence Shaw, Constable, and John Foster, John Wright of Oakworth, and John Shackleton of Newsholme, Church-wardens, who made distress as follows:—

	£.	s.	d.
"Taken from Thomas Brigg, one mugg, pewter dish and tanker, worth	0	13	0
Richard Waddington, pewter,	0	7	4
James Ramsden, 220 lbs. of oat meal,	0	18	4
John Hird, pewter,	0	4	8
Jeremy Brigg, pewter,	0	7	0
John and William Smith, a vice, a coat and money,	1	8	6

The Quakers have long since ceased to exist as a religious society in Keighley; and the small chapel in Mill-lane (now Old Bridge-street,) which we believe still belongs to the general body, is occasionally occupied as a school-room. They had a small burying-ground attached to the chapel, and another called the 'Sepulchre,' used by some of the more wealthy families, situated at Calversyke-hill.*

---

* Calver, from Calfherd; syke, a water-course—it sometimes means a slow or boggy brook. Or did a person named Calfere, or Calvert, once own this part of the syke? We don't think the first part is from calvus, bald or bare.

There is also an old grave-yard at Cross Flatts, which belonged to the Mauds of Castlefield and Friends about Bingley.

The family of Richard Shackleton of Harden, who was fined upwards of £10. for attending the meeting at Stubbing House, subsequently settled in Ireland; and we feel pretty confident that it was one of his descendants, a schoolmaster, who had the honour of teaching the celebrated Burke, and whose son, a learned correspondent of the *Gentlemen's Magazine*, was the friend and companion of that great orator and statesman. Their former residence, a substantial old building in Harden, is still called 'Shackleton House.'

WESLEYAN METHODISTS.

THE annexed account of the laying of the foundation-stone, and summary of Methodism in Keighley, appeared in one of the provincial journals:—

"The foundation-stone of the Wesleyan Methodist Chapel, Keighley, was laid on Monday, the 28th day of July, in the ninth year of the reign of Her Majesty Queen Victoria, and in the year of our Lord, 1845, by Lodge Calvert of Bradford, Gent.

Joseph Rayner, John Hanson, William J. Skidmore, } Circuit Ministers.		John Laycock, William Thomas, } Circuit Stewards.

"This new chapel stands upon the site of the first Methodist Chapel erected in Keighley, which was built in 1754—rebuilt, 1777; and upon the erection of Eden Chapel in 1810, was converted into a Sunday School. Its Trustees are—

Mr. Lodge Calvert,	Mr. Thomas Waterhouse,	Mr. Samuel Smith,
Thomas Pearson,	Thomas Midgley,	John Holmes,
Nathan Holmes,	John Craven,	Jonas Sugden,
John Laycock,	William Thomas,	Nathaniel Walbank.

"The members of the building committee are Mr. Samuel B. Clapham, Mr. Edmund Laycock, Mr. William Lund and the Town Trustees.

"This stone was laid in the 106th year of the existence of Wesleyan Methodism, and the 103rd year of its introduction into Keighley. The Rev. Jabez Bunting, D. D., being the President, and the Rev. Robert Newton, D.D., the Secretary of the Conference.

"The Sabbath School, which was re-established in 1807, and is well arranged, contains 711 children, and is conducted gratuitously by two presidents, eight superintendents and 106 teachers. The Day School, conducted on the Glasgow system by one master and two mistresses, instructs upwards of 250 children.

"Lodge Calvert of Bradford, Gent. (being the only trustee living on the enlargement of the first erection), officiated in laying the stone, which was preceded by an affecting prayer from the Rev. J. Hanson of Haworth, and followed by an address from the Rev. J. Skidmore, who after having read the inscriptions on the plates, proceeded to comment on the early days of Methodism in Keighley, and traced its infant commencement from three members, who constituted the society here in 1742, and which by regular steps have increased to 1778 in 103 years. The Rev. J. Everett of York and the Rev. J. Rayner also addressed the assembly at some length, on the gratifying fact that

Methodism instead of retrograding, as some parties had gratuitously asserted, was increasing in numbers, which was a novel sign of going backwards."

This circuit has been comparatively free from the great defections which have recently signalized the history of Methodism; it now numbers about 2000 members, 40 local preachers and 100 class meetings; in fact it is one of the most prosperous circuits in the kingdom.

SWEDENBORGIANS.

The Swedenborgian religion, which stands next in chronological order, was introduced into this town by the late Rev. Robert Hindmarsh, whose sister married Mr. William Illingworth, a gentleman of this place. Mr. Hindmarsh was one of a number of young men in London, who first began to consider the Swedish Philosopher as the founder of a new sect, undertaking to translate his works, and eagerly propagating the new doctrine. In 1805, when their present place of worship was erected, they appear to have been in a state of considerable prosperity. At present they have no stated services, though in possession of a small income from freehold property intended for the support of a minister.

BAPTISTS.

The Baptist Interest, to adopt their peculiar phraseology, was established in 1809, by the late Mr. John Town and a few friends who were chiefly members of the Baptist Chapel at Haworth. Their temporary accommodations proving inadequate to the wants of an increasing congregation, they erected the present neat little chapel, which was opened in 1815. They have generally a resident minister, but when there is a vacancy, as now, service is performed by students from Horton College. We believe their experience has been, like that of most infant societies, chequered by sunshine and shade.

METHODISTS' NEW CONNEXION.

That section of the Methodist body called the 'New Connexion,' or 'Kilhamites,' built a chapel, and seemed to prosper in Keighley for a number of years. But owing to the imprudence of some of its trustees and leading members, the society gradually fell away until they were unable to support a minister and maintain the cause; they then sold the chapel, and sought among other congregations of the town for such spiritual fellowship and worship as they had hitherto enjoyed together. This building, which stands in South-street, was lately used as a coach-maker's shop, and it is now converted into shops and cottages.

PRIMITIVE METHODISTS.

On Sunday, Sep, 16th, 1821, whilst the Primitive Methodists, whose doctrines had been recently introduced into this town, were holding a lovefeast in a large room belonging to Mr. Richard Hattersley, at Mill-hill, the floor suddenly gave way and precipitated them into a dark and dusty apartment below, where from fifty to sixty persons were severely crushed and wounded. One of them died on the following day, and eleven had broken bones. This, though a very distressing, was a somewhat ludicrous scene; many returning to their distant homes, though happily unhurt, yet looking extremely comical, and so much disfigured in their outward appearance as to be hardly known by their astonished and sympathising neighbours. The lamentable occurrence was made the subject of a printed poem by Mr. J. Jowett, entitled "The Disaster."

As a proof of the progress of this body of Christians we may add that they afterwards built a chapel in Sun-street, which proving too small, they erected the present handsome and commodious chapel in Queen-street, where divine service is now performed.

The Wesleyan Association Methodists, who seceded from the 'Old Body' in 1828, in consequence of an organ dispute at Leeds, built a chapel in Sun-street, in which they now worship. They have very recently united with the Wesleyan Reformers, under the name of the "United Methodist Free Churches."

The Roman Catholics hired a room for service in South-street, in 1832; and about the year 1836 built their present chapel. We are not aware that they have made any converts among the English, but as there are some hundreds of resident Irish they muster a goodly congregation on the sabbath day.

Omitting the three churches, the places of worship belonging to the different denominations of Christians in Keighley stand in the following Chronological order:—

> The Independent Chapel.
> Wesleyan Methodist Chapel, Temple-street.
> Swedenborgian Chapel, King-street, Clubhouses.
> Baptist Chapel, Baptist-square, High-street.
> Primitive Methodist Chapel, Queen-street.
> Wesleyan Association Chapel, Sun-street.
> St. Anne's Catholic Chapel, Flush, Skipton-road.

THE MECHANICS' INSTITUTION.

The Keighley Mechanics' Institution, if not one of the most flourishing, is certainly one of the oldest in the north of England. The following somewhat vivid account of its origin and early progress may be seen in the Second Annual Report:—" Four individuals had met at one of their habitations for social intercourse, one of whom had fortunately met with a periodical publication* which described the establishment and progress of a society formed by the operatives of the Gas Company in Glasgow. This account was read to the other three, and as the description proceeded the impressions were so remarkably reciprocal that ere its conclusion their feelings were so enthusiastic on the subject that the little group resolved to unite in a similar cause. Although their own spirits had been so readily and powerfully excited, yet their most sanguine expectations were so limited, that they had no idea that more than a dozen might be united with them in so novel an undertaking. One of them was speedily appointed chairman, a second secretary, and they and the other two constituted themselves a committee, and passed several resolutions relative to the future state of the society. They informed only a narrow sphere of acquaintance with their design, announcing the time of their next meeting, at which they were exceedingly surprised by the attendance of a great number, all desirous of uniting with them, and willing to promote the advancement of the infant institution.

---

* "The Mechanics' Magazine," vol. 1st, page 161.

It was therefore expedient that they should assemble in a larger room. An application was made to the Trustees of the Free Grammar School, soliciting the use of that building, which was offered with a promptitude that reflected the highest credit upon them. A Library was established, which was soon considerably augmented by the liberal donations and presents of many respectable individuals of the town and its vicinity, whose kindness the committee will at all times be prompt to acknowledge, giving as it did an important impulse to their own exertions."

The four persons who formed the nucleus of the society, and who may be considered its original promoters, were John Farish, a reed-maker, John Bradley, a painter, William Dixon, a tailor, and John Haigh, a joiner; and the subjoined is copied verbatim from a written circular issued on that occasion to the writer of this account.

"Sir,—At a meeting held at Mr. Farish's to form a society for mutual instruction, and to establish a library for that purpose, it was unanimously resolved that cards of invitation should be sent to all persons likely to become members thereof.

"You are hereby requested to attend at Mr. Farish's house, on Monday evening, January 24th inst., at eight o'clock, in order to enrol yourself (if you think proper) a member thereof, and to assist in making rules for the government thereof.

"Upper Green,   "JOHN BRADLEY,
"Jan. 22nd, 1825.   "Secretary."

Though it is evident that the first meeting of this institution was on the 24th of January, it has been usual to date its establishment from a public meeting held in the National School-room at Mill Hill, on the 14th of February, 1825. This meeting was called for the purpose of adopting the rules, giving publicity to its proceedings and sanction to the principles on which it was founded.

The Hall of the Mechanics' Institution, which cost according to the account of the building committee, £1043. 7s. 6d., was erected in 1834, and is held by fifteen trustees under a lease for sixty years of the Earl of Burlington, at the ground rent of £2. per annum. The Earl of Burlington is patron of the Institution, and the annexed is a list of the names on the original trustees.

> Rev. Theodore Dury, M.A., (late Rector).
> William Ellis, Esq., Castle Field.
> Frederick Greenwood, Esq., Ryshworth Hall.
> Edwin Greenwood, Esq., Knoll, Keighley.
> Christopher Netherwood, Esq., Cliffe Hall.
> William Sugden, Esq., Eastwood House.
> Samuel Blakey Clapham, Esq., Aireworth House.
> Mr. Benjamin Flesher Marriner. Mr. Thomas Mills.
> Mr. John Craven. Mr. John Brigg.
> Mr. John Laycock. Mr. John Farish.
> Mr. Michael Craven. Mr. William Blake.

The present state and efficiency of this Institution will be best explained by the introduction of a portion of the Report just published for the year ending March 31st, 1857, by which it appears that the number of members amounts to 274; the number of volumes in the library, to 2,708, their total circulation during the year to 8,680, or about three times for each volume—five volumes have been presented and 133 purchased during the same period. The gross receipts for the year, including a former balance, are £197. 6s.; and after paying all expenses the balance in hand is £15. 6s. The classes in operation are Drawing, Grammar, Writing and Arithmetic. In the reading-room there are 12 newspapers and 12 periodicals. In the savings' bank, which is kept on the same premises, there are now 690 depositors.

To those who have had the misfortune to receive only the wretched modicum of education doled out to the poor in this country, Mechanics' Institutions must be of the utmost importance; and such as have not yet been able to see in their steady and successful career, "that the march of intellect and the walking abroad of the schoolmaster are something more than things to furnish a joke or a witticism, are blind indeed to the signs of the times, and to the certainty that the spread of sound knowledge amongst the people will yet make this nation more deserving of the epithet of a nation of princes than ever Rome deserved from the Parthian ambassador."

In furtherance of the cause of education and the diffusion of social and political information several periodical papers have at different times been published here, but for want of encouragement their existence has generally been of short duration. The *Keighley Visitor*, a semi-Temperance monthly, and the *Keighley and Skipton Mercury*, a weekly political, are our present organs of public opinion.

Additional to the buildings already noticed are several handsome shops, inns, and public rooms, on sites giving greater uniformity and width to the streets, and whose general appearance has an air of neatness and taste commensurate with the advancing importance of the town. It would, we think, be highly conducive to the weal and sanitary condition of the inhabitants, if the great attention now given to convenience and health in cottage-erections should be the means of stopping the further increase of cellar abodes.

Before the impulse recently given by manufactures to our progress in population and wealth we had only one superior mansion to greet the eye of the traveller as he entered the town, viz., Knoll or Knowle House, on the south-west, erected with a regard to comfort rather than to ornament, by the father of that worthy and wealthy gentleman, the late John Greenwood, Esq,; it is now occupied by Mr. William Lund, Worsted Manufacturer. The editor distinctly remembers with what glee in his school-boy days he used to peep through the thinner parts of a privet-hedge which crowned the low wall by which the place was then separated from the Halifax road, and hopefully anticipate the time when his increased stature would enable him to peer at the 'fine hall' over hedge and wall as he passed along the road; but just upon the consummation of his boyish hopes, the low fence was replaced by one of such huge proportions as effectually frustrated his fond anticipations, and left him to muse on the vanity of human wishes.

Several new halls and villas now adorn our neighbourhood; and a series of handsome houses commencing at the Bank, the most elegant edifice in the town, and continued at intervals to a considerable distance on the north-road, has a fair claim to the epithet, the 'West End,' in the aristocratic sense. In this direction stands Cliffe Hall, a light, ornate structure, in the Elizabethan style, and surrounded by a grove of trees enclosing pleasant gardens. It is now the property and residence of John Butterfield, Esq., of the firm of Butterfield Brothers, Merchants and extensive Worsted Manufacturers. Beech Cliffe, a plain, commodious house to the north, the residence of Mr. Joseph Smith, demands a cursory notice from the extensive views which it commands over the valley of the Aire, while its situation near an angle of the north-road, and just within the southern point of a crescent-formed portion of ground which swells up in the rear to a considerable height, agreeably shuts out of sight the smoky atmosphere of the town, and gives the place an air of seclusion from its busy scenes. A little beyond Spring Gardens, the quiet abode of Benjamin F. Marriner, Esq., is Prospect House, romantically perched on a part of the above-mentioned crescent-formed ground as steep as the roof that covers the fabric. Unfortunately, wood, the choicest element in nature's painting, is here but scantily bestowed. A good plantation of full-grown trees and evergreen under-wood encircling this house would add materially to its comfort and beauty, and leave a pleasing impression upon the mind of the beholder, enhanced by contrast with the naked aspect of the background; and we notice that its owner, Mr. Thomas Wall, Wine and Spirit Merchant, has begun on a small scale to supply by art what nature has denied. On the very brow of this eminence is a good house, built, it is said, for the threefold purpose of enjoying the distant views and bracing air of this upland region, and the *not* very peculiar whim of excluding every mill-chimney from the sight of its occupant.

Eastwood House, which, as its name implies, is situated to the east of the town on a spacious area of even ground environed by a fine plantation of trees, and near to the pleasant Aire, which here sweeps placidly in a deep bed through the rich plain of the valley, is perhaps the largest family residence in the vicinity. The stone of which it is composed is of good quality, retains its colour well, and is of that peculiar cast which gives the idea of comfort. It baffles our skill to determine its predominating style of architecture, though we think it partakes of the Doric order. It is the residence of John G. Sugden, Esq., Magistrate; and it was built in 1819 by his respected father, the late William Sugden, Esq. Aireworth, still more eastward, the plain comfortable dwelling of Samuel B. Clapham, Esq., Worsted Manufacturer, is too closely embosomed by the foliage of a tuft of trees to be easily seen.

The best modern building to our liking is Worthville, the Elizabethan seat of William Marriner, Esq. In a few years the more mature growth of the surrounding shrubs and trees will complete the attractions of this admirably-situated villa, and render it the most striking object in the landscape. We rarely look upon it without thinking that its position is alike suitable for the philanthropist to refresh his thoughts, and warm his heart with purposes of love to his fellow-man as he gazes on the thriving town which nestles at the foot of the hill, or for the student of nature to furnish his mind with sweet reflections on the beauties of creation, as he contemplates the diversified and picturesque scenery in the distance.

ARMORIAL BEARINGS OF THE NEIGHBOURING GENTRY, 1857.

FERRAND.

THE Ferrands of St. Ives and Harden Grange, parish of Bingley, bear or, on a chief gu, two crosses patence, vair. Crest, a cubit arm, erect, rested vair;

cuff, or, holding in the hand, ppr, a battle-axe of the second.

BUSFEILD.

The Rev. William Busfeild, M. A., Rector, and Rural Dean, nephew and heir of the late respected William Busfeild, Esq., of Upwood, M. P. for the borough of Bradford, sable, a chevron between three flowers de lis, or.

GARFORTH.

Thomas Garforth, Esq., of Steeton, sa, a bend between six goats passant, az. Crest, out of a ducal coronet, az., a goat's head of the last.

GREENWOOD.

Frederick Greenwood, Esq., late of Knowle House, Keighley, and Ryshworth Hall, Bingley, now of Norton Conyers, Ripon, sable, a chevron ermines, between three saltires, argent.

SUGDEN.

John Greenwood Sugden, Esq., of Eastwood House, arg., a fesse, or, in chief three women's heads, couped at the shoulders, ppr, vested and crined, or, in base, a leopard's head of the last. Crest, a leopard's head, erased, or, ducally gorged azure.

ELLIS.

William Ellis, Esq., of Castlefield, or, on a cross, sable, five crescents, argent, with another for a difference, in the first canton. Crest, on a chapeau gules, crined ermine, a lion rampant, or.

TRADE AND MANUFACTURES.

The early introduction of spinning machinery, and the subsequent prosperity of this town, are due to the two becks or rivulets which mingle their waters at Calepit and discharge their joint contents into the river Aire about a mile below. Hence the two streams, with their sparkling feeders trickling down the sides of the adjacent hills like the tears of the Naiads shed in view of the unrural offices which await them, are entitled to our consideration as the principal sources of wealth, not only to the mill-owners on their banks, but to the tradesmen and landed proprietors of the surrounding district. For as the number of revolving spindles has continued to increase, the bleak and sterile hills have been gradually yielding to the determined and persevering arm of the cultivator; and the augmented crops of cereals and herbage from the rich loamy soil on the east and north of the town are also due to the same stimulating energies. In "Harrison's description of Britaine," prefixed to "Holinshead's Chronicle," first edition, 1577, they are designated the "Worthe" and the "Laccoc," evidently from Haworth and Laycock, the two places of most note in the direction of their commencement, but we believe the popular title of the two streams to have been in Harrison's time as at present the Sun Beck and the North Beck. Facilities for crossing these useful streams are numerous, as in and near the town no less than fourteen stone bridges may be enumerated. In respect to its trade, Keighley was for a long time dependent upon Halifax, first vending its woollens and then its worsted goods in that market. But since the decline of the figured stuffs called Drawboys, Bradford has become the principal market town, and considerable intercourse is kept up between the two places. That this town was early engaged in the making of woollen cloth, will be evident from the following entry in the parish register:—"John Hartley, a Clothier, buried 29th December, 1571;" and March, 1738—9, the death of Thomas Brook, the Fulling Miller, is mentioned; and there are places not only in Keighley, but in the village of Laycock, bearing the name of "Tenter Croft." But some time previous to the death of the Fulling Miller, we find that the worsted or shalloon trade had begun to take root in the neighbourhood, as the following evidence adduced from the same source will show:—"Peter Hall, Yarn Dealer, and John Slater, Shalloon Maker, buried, 1724; Abraham Binns, Wool-comb Maker, 1725; Jonas Blakey, Shalloon Maker, 1744; Matthew Barwick and Thomas Keighley, Shalloon Makers, 1749." It has also been found in letters still preserved by a respectable and long established manufacturing firm in this town, that one of their ancestors was sending worsted pieces direct to London in 1724, to be disposed of by an agent of the name of Leach.

The following copy of an indenture gives us a favourable opinion of the character of our early clothiers; it also informs us negatively of the prevailing temptations and sins of the young men of that day:—

"This Indenture, made the 1st September, 1671, between John Barrett, of Laycock, Clothier, on the one part, and I, Joseph, son of Anthony Wright, Yeoman, of Laycock, on the other part, Witnesseth, that J. Wright, of his own free and voluntary will, and with the consent and good liking had and obtained of his friends, hath put and bound himself apprentice to the said J. Barrett, to dwell and remain with him for 7 years, to be taught the art or trade of woollen webster, which is used in the house of J. Barrett. He,

J. Wright, shall faithfully serve his honest commands, shall do no damage to his master, and suffer none to be done, not to go to tavern and alehouses, or give way to incontinence or fornication; he shall not play at cards or dice; he shall not depart or absent himself without leave of his master, &c. To have eleven shillings in the first five years, thirteen in the sixth, and sixteen in the seventh year, and a pair of hose yearly, with sufficient meat, drink, lodging, washing, &c.

"Signed,
"ANTHONY WRIGHT.
"JOSEPH WRIGHT.
"JOHN BARRETT."

The woollen trade appears to have taken its final departure soon after the middle of the last century, and the old Fulling or Walker's Mill, which stood on the premises now occupied by the Messrs. Craven, called "Walk Mill,"* was turned into a silk-mill, by that ingenious and enterprising gentleman, Mr. Joseph Stell, who is said to have woven silk tapes and other narrow fabrics by water power. Unfortunately for this individual and his family, in an evil hour he was induced to overstep the line of moral rectitude, and plunge into a sea of trouble and distress. He suffered at York for counterfeiting the gold coin of the realm, and his estate was confiscated to the crown. In the anonymous "History of Halifax," published, 1789, the shalloon trade is said to have been introduced into that place "about the beginning of the present century, and what are called figured stuffs or drawboys within the compass of a few years." Hence it might appear that this parish was equally as forward as Halifax; and from the time of the expulsion of the woollen to the introduction of cotton, more completely absorbed in the worsted trade than either Halfax or Bradford.

As the centre of a district, Keighley continued for

---

* Walk-mill and Fulling-mill are synonymous.

some time to keep up its grand septennial procession in commemoration of Bishop Blaise, the reputed patron of wool-combers; but these gaudy spectacles are now discontinued, being considered extravagant and foolish.

Before the invention of spinning machinery, the manufacturer of worsted goods often experienced much difficulty in procuring yarn in sufficient quantities to supply the loom of the weaver, and was even in ordinary times obliged to have recourse to the wheels of the distant villages. In brisk and prosperous times the produce of the widest and most extensive districts was found inadequate to the demand. Whilst the worsted trade continued in this state, apparently limited in quantity and extent, a new and important era had commenced in the cotton trade. The time had now arrived when

> "Arkwright's genius pierced the rugged glen,
> Made sterile places busy haunts of men,
> Plac'd in our vale the pond'rous water-wheel
> To draw each thread, and urge the whirling steel."

The large cotton-mill, called "Low Mill," begun by the Ramsdens of Halifax, and completed by Messrs. Clayton and Walshman, gentlemen from Lancashire, first commenced running on the 30th of June, 1780. The machinery was made under the directions of Sir Richard Arkwright, and as it was the first cotton-mill ever erected in this county, the proprietors found themselves under the necessity of sending a number of children and young persons to Sir Richard's works, at Cromford in Derbyshire, to learn the business. From this time the gentlemen and yeomen of the parish, the Greenwoods, the Blakeys, the Ellises, the

the Smiths, the Cravens, the Briggs and other families allured by the hopes of gain, began to appropriate the valuable waterfalls and eligible mill-sites, and venture their capital in the new and popular speculation, so that by 1805, when Dr. Whitaker paid his first visit, there were no less than ten cotton factories in and about the town. This hideous and repulsive sight elicited from the courteous and enlightened historian the following remarks:—" This parish lies immediately north from that of Bingley in the course of the Aire, with little that can interest the eye, the memory, or the imagination. I may therefore be excused if I betray some anxiety to reach more pleasing scenes, for hard is the fate of the topographer while he respires the smoke of manufactures, and is stunned by the din of recent population." Some historians make a great parade about their impartiality,— not so the Doctor: he seems to have considered an openly avowed prejudice to be a sufficient excuse for the neglect of duty. Low Mill is now the property of John Craven, Esq., Magistrate, where he and his sons having made considerable additions to the premises, carry on an extensive worsted business.

Although the cotton trade at this period appears to have taken full possession of the district, the worsted business had already begun to rally, and was now seen to be slowly and steadily improving. Owing to the wide difference in the nature of sheep's wool and cotton, it was sometime before the new principle of spinning by rollers could be successfully applied in the former case. But this great object was at length accomplished, and the new machinery properly adapted to the nature of the raw material, as we are informed in Nicholson's "Operative Mechanic," by

Mr. Hargreaves of Addingham, who succeeded to such an extent as to induce Messrs. William Birkbeck & Co. of Settle to build a large mill at Linton, where the application of the new principle of spinning by rollers was successfully carried out. About this time, or soon after, the hand-throstle was invented by two individuals of this town, John Weatherhead, a joiner, and John Nicholson, afterwards a printer in Bradford. This valuable machine, which was at first made single and turned by hand, required only to be made double, and propelled by water or steam-power, to become what it is at present, the worsted spinning-frame or the cotton throstle. Viewed as an improvement of the old water frame, it consisted principally in the coupling together of the rollers and the introduction of a tin cylinder of corresponding length, by means of which only one set of wheels or gearing was required for the whole length of the frame, whilst in the former machine separate gearing was necessary for every four or six spindles. The cylinder, being made to drive the rollers, gives motion to the spindles and twist to the thread.

Under the head "Spinning," in the "Encyclopædia Britannica," seventh edition, the value of the improvement is thus estimated:—"One of the greatest improvements of modern days is the simplification of the moving parts, by making each roller continuous along the whole length of the machine, and using only one set of driving apparatus at the one or other extremity, and by making the shaft for driving the twisting machinery also continuous, as will be seen in the drawing of the frame for flax spinning." In fact this improvement constituted an epoch in the history of spinning machinery marked by a considerable saving in power and expense.

Whilst water continued the principal element of power, Keighley appears to have taken the lead in the spinning department, but no sooner had the steam-engine begun to be planted over the rich coal-beds of Bradford and Halifax, than it was again left in the rear. Yet notwithstanding its less favourable position with respect to coal, this town still maintains its rank as the head of the third division of the Yorkshire Worsted District, carrying on as an auxiliary or minor branch of trade, the making of woolcombs, slays, healds and spinning machinery. It is now noted for the manufacture of rollers, spindles, flyers and other materials used in spinning, and the making of machinery.

The quantity of wool consumed in Keighley in the year 1839, as stated in the "History of Bradford," from returns of the drawback on soap, was 4,293,120 ℔s.

The following is a correct statement of the amount of drawback on soap consumed by the worsted manufacturers, 1843, in the undermentioned districts:—

Bradford district	....	£5,008.
Halifax	,, ...	£4,552.
Keighley	,, ...	£2,704.

The comparative degree of perfection now attained in the construction of combing-machines has induced many of our manufacturers to substitute those machines for hand-combing; and, as is always the case in every department of trade when mechanical appliances are superseding hand-labour, the transition state of the combing business in Keighley entails a great amount of suffering upon the unfortunate wool-combers.

In 1850, the official returns of the factory inspectors showed that there were then employed within the walls of the various mills in Keighley, 4460 persons; and in an interesting lecture delivered in London during the Exhibition, 1851, by Mr. Forbes of Bradford, he reckons fifty per cent. more for those employed out of the factories, which, so far as Keighley is concerned, is probably below the mark.

There are at present about 31 worsted mills and several weaving sheds in this parish, where a brisk and lucrative business is carried on by about 30 firms; besides which there are 4 small mills empty. As an approximate estimate of the amount of work done, we may state that they employ about 82,000 spindles, 3,050 power-looms and 30 combing machines.

STATISTICAL REMARKS.

To our highly-esteemed antiquarian friend, Mr. Jonathan Hindle, we stand indebted for the following statistical particulars drawn from the Parish Register.

"In the course of thirteen years ending 1812, when the population of the parish amounted to 6,364, there were buried 120 persons of 70 and under 80 years of age; 42 of 80 and under 90; and 8 varying from 90 to 100.

"In the Register for 1593, Adam Widdop was buried, aged 100 years; 1625, Dennis Garforth, aged 103; and in 1656, Henry Wright, 100.

"The most healthy years are 1587, 1588, 1589, 1590 and 1591, which did not average more than 10 deaths annually, whilst the five preceding years amounted to 16, and the five subsequent, to 24 yearly. 1623 is the year when the greatest mortality prevailed, the average of five years previous being 31, whilst in that year no less than 112 are recorded; assuming the then population at 1330, which number is rather above than below the mark, it will be one death

STATISTICS. 113

in 12, or near four times the usual number. We likewise find, on comparing the relative number of deaths in each month, that April, and after that May, are the most fatal to human life, and the months of September and October the least so. The number of deaths in the April months from 1562 to 1812, embracing a period of 250 years (including ten that are illegible), amount to 1296, whilst in the months of September during the same time they amounted only to 900.

"On looking over the number of births during the time of Queen Elizabeth we do not find any increase, but on the contrary, they appear to have retrograded towards the latter end of that reign. Under the sway of the pacific James and part of the reign of Charles I., in a period of forty years ending 1643, they had augmented at least sixty per cent.; but in the next twenty years Keighley was visited with two of the greatest scourges that can afflict the human race—war and pestilence. The consequence was a considerable diminution in the quantity of births, as may be seen by referring to the foregoing tables, [the tables here referred to may be seen in a manuscript presented by the person before noticed to the Library of the Keighley Mechanics' Institution] and it was not till near the lapse of a century that this parish recovered from the two-fold calamity.

"In the reign of the first George, we again find a gradual improvement in the number of births, and it would seem that about this time trade was introduced into this place, or at least considerably extended, combers and weavers being now for the first time mentioned in the Register. This conjecture is sufficiently confirmed by the fact of the births having

114   STATISTICS.

been nearly doubled in the course of forty years, the increase of population depending upon trade and the increased means of procuring subsistence."

In the year 1675 this town was visited by that fatal epidemic profanely called 'The Jolly Rant.' "This disorder was accompanied with a severe cold and violent cough, which prevailed to such an extent, and affected people so universally, that during Divine service it was almost impossible to hear distinctly a single sentence of the sermon." In that year the number of deaths amounted to 105, whilst the regular average was under 40.

Though we have no positive account of the number of inhabitants in this parish in the reign of Elizabeth, it is quite certain that either its sanitary state was good or that the population was very low indeed. It will be found in the Register that the average of deaths for a period of 40 years did not amount to more than 20 annually: hence, assuming that only 1 in 50, or two per cent., died in each year, and multiplying 50 by 20, the mean average of the forty years' deaths, we derive only 1,000 for the population of the parish at that time, an approximation most likely very near the truth.

According to the account of Parson Gale, as stated at page 51, this town in the year 1695 consisted of 100 houses; and the parish, upon an exact enumeration, was found to contain 1,704 inhabitants. If we divide this number by the mean average of deaths for 21 years, ten preceding and ten succeeding the above date, the result of the operation will show that 1 out of every $45\frac{24}{31}$ died annually at that period. From the six official returns of the census, the advancement of the population of this parish since the commencement of the present century may be thus exhibited :—

The number of inhabitants in 1801 amounted to 5,745
,, ,, 1811 ,, 6,864
,, ,, 1821 ,, 9,223
,, ,, 1831 ,, 11,176
,, ,, 1841 ,, 13,378
,, ,, 1851 ,, 18,258

From this data, with the aid of the Parish Register and the District Registrar's accounts, it has been ascertained that on an average of 50 years, that is from 1801 to 1851, about 1 in 47 died annually.

In 1808 the town contained 786 houses, 13 of which were public-houses, the parish church and three chapels, with a population, reckoning five in a house, of 3,930. In 1846 it was found to contain, with Calversyke hill and Thwaites, 8,840, and in 1851, according to the government account, 13,050. But as it is probable from the number of inhabitants here returned, that the limits of the town had been too much restricted, the annexed statement may afford a more satisfactory precedent in that respect for the time to come.

May 27th, 1853, when on the re-establishment of the Street-gas Rate, the number of occupied dwellings was required to be known, there were found to be within the limits of the Town Improvements Act, or, in other words, within a circle the radius of which is a mile and its centre the Old Market-place, 2,930. Hence, by multiplying this number by $5\frac{1}{4}$, the average per house throughout the union in 1851, the town defined as above was found to contain 15,382 inhabitants. It is worthy of remark, as a fact ominous to the tallow-chandler, that the quantity of gas consumed within this area in the year ending July, 1857, was 12,000,000 cubic feet.

We are not aware of the existence of any documents containing a reliable account of the rates of wages paid to the husbandmen and artizans of the town and parish in olden times, but we may reasonably infer that they would be rather lower than those paid to the same classes in more populous seats of industry. The accompanying table of poor-rates levied in this parish, with the population, price of corn per qr., and assessment per head, may mislead us in attempting to estimate the relative well-being of the people at the periods stated, if we omit to notice that in 1730, when our table begins, the wages of a husbandman were about 4s. or 5s. per week, and of an artizan 8s. to 10s., and that wheat-corn was little used here before the commencement of the present century.

Average of 5 years.	Poor Rates. £. s. d.	Population.	Per Head. s. d.	Price of Corn. £. s. d.
Year Ending 1730	152 15 11	2160	1 4½	2 2 0
,, 1735	178 1 8	2310	1 6½	1 10 10
,, 1740	194 9 6	2490	1 8½	1 14 1
,, 1745	288 15 1	2660	2 2	1 8 1
,, 1750	244 13 1	2845	1 8½	1 12 1
,, 1755	289 13 1	3045	2 2½	1 14 5
,, 1760	383 2 0	3235	2 4½	2 0 9
,, 1765	441 8 0	3450	2 6½	1 17 5
,, 1770	472 6 0	3650	2 7	2 7 8
,, 1775	678 11 8	3880	3 6	2 14 11
,, 1780	770 13 0	4100	3 9	2 2 10
,, 1785	903 2 6	4340	4 2	2 13 6
,, 1790	738 8 3	4645	3 2	2 9 11
,, 1795	997 14 5	5120	3 11	2 18 8
,, 1801	1447 11 0	5745	5 0	4 7 11
,, 1806	1622 11 5	6250	5 2	3 13 6
,, 1811	1796 12 7	6864	5 3	4 14 7
,, 1816	2078 5 2	7870	5 3	4 18 2
,, 1821	2185 5 7	9223	4 8	4 7 10
,, 1826	2187 19 1	10210	4 3	3 7 10
,, 1831	2466 18 10	11309	4 4	3 6 4
,, 1836	2650 18 1	12290	4 4	2 8 6

We cannot vouch for the accuracy of the above prices

of corn, as all the tables which we have examined differ from one another.

The rates collected in the year 1850, amounted to £3,295. 5s. 9¼d.; those in 1854, when trade was bad and food dear, to about £5,820. 16s.

INCREASE OF THE SMITHS.

"Whence cometh Smyth, albe he knight or squire,
But from the smith that smiteth at the fire."

WHETHER the Smiths of this parish, as is apprehended of some kinds of fish in certain rivers, are destined in the course of time to swallow and absorb the rest, the writer does not venture to predict; but an acquaintance with the following facts may perhaps enable the curious observer to determine with some degree of accuracy their future progress as compared with the rest of the population. In the reign of Queen Elizabeth, when the population was about 1,000, Smith does not appear to have been the most common surname; yet in 1846, it was ascertained from the ratebook that whilst the whole number of occupied dwellings amounted to 2,983, with a population of about 15,000, no less than 204 were found to be in the possession of the Smiths, which multiplied by five gives 1,020 persons to this very prolific family, being as one to fifteen, in 1846, or equal to the whole population of the parish in the flourishing days of Elizabeth. Though one branch of this family have a tradition that their original surname was Shoesmith, it will probably be found on inspection that neither Shoesmith, Goldsmith, Arrowsmith, nor any of that class of names ever found a place in the Parish Register.

118   POLLING STATION—POOR LAW UNION.

After the Smiths, the following table, which we made a few years ago, may be regarded as a correct list of some of the most common surnames, with the number of families belonging to each :—

Sugden 68	Binns......... 43	Sharp 34
Shackleton ... 52	Heaton 43	Hartley 39
Moore............ 52	Holmes 43	Naylor 19
Butterfield ... 50	Midgley...... 37	Craven 18
Wright 45	Hey............ 35	Clapham 16

KEIGHLEY MADE A POLLING STATION.

On the passing of the Boundary Act, in connexion with the Reform Bill, which was granted in 1832, Keighley was made a polling town or station, comprehending within its district the following places :— the two parishes of Keighley and Bingley, the township of Haworth in the parish of Bradford, with the several townships of Sutton, Steeton-cum-Eastburn and Silsden in the parish of Kildwick. In 1841 the number of registered voters in the Keighley polling district amounted to 1,316. By a new regulation, which took effect in 1855, all the above places, excepting Haworth, were severed from Keighley. The number of voters for the year 1857 in the two united places is 818 ; 570 belonging to Keighley, and 248 to Haworth. In the new polling station of Bingley, with its associated township of Morton, there are 438 voters.

THE KEIGHLEY UNION.

The Keighley Union, as collected from the Third Annual Report of the Poor Law Commissioners was declared to take place from and after the 10th of February, 1836.

PLACES UNITED.	Population in 1831.	No. of Guardians.
1—Keighley	11,176	6
2—Bingley with Micklethwaite	8,036	4
3—East and West Morton	1,219	1
4—Haworth	5,853	3
5—Steeton with Eastburn	859	1
6—Sutton	1,153	1
Total	28,296	16

In 1841 this Union contained 36,175 inhabitants. In 1851 it contained 8,649 inhabited houses, 45,749 persons, 22,659 males and 23,090 females, the number of Guardians continuing as before. Silsden, though at that time in the Keighley polling and Registrar's district, was not in the Keighley Union, it having previous to the establishment of the latter belonged to a Gilbert's Union, held at Carlton near Otley, and it still belongs to it.

THE BURSTING OF CROW-HILL BOG,

WITH ANNALS OF THE TOWN'S FURTHER PROGRESS.

In 1752 the Act for Making and Improving the Keighley and Kendal Turnpike Road was granted. In 1780 an Act of Parliament was obtained for the Inclosure of Waste Lands within the parish; and in 1816 an Act was obtained for Supplying the Town with Water. The Savings' bank was established in 1819; and it is open at the Mechanics' Institution on the first, second, and third Saturdays of each month from five to seven o'clock in the evening, and on the second Wednesday of every month from one to two;

Mr. Edward Metcalfe is its Secretary. The deposits amounted in November, 1851, to £40,589. belonging to 1,459 depositors, and 29 charitable and friendly societies. In 1824 the royal assent was given to an Act for Lighting and Improving the town. On the 2nd of September of the same year the inhabitants on the banks of the river Aire were greatly alarmed by the disruption of a bog at Crow-hill above Haworth, in a wild part of the county adjoining to Lancashire, which kept the water of the river Aire in such a turbid state that for some time it could not be used at Leeds or any other place, either for culinary or manufacturing purposes. Three days after the commencement of the disruption, the Rev. Mr. Bronte of Haworth sent a letter to the *Leeds Mercury* office stating that he believed it to be the effects of a severe earthquake; but as no agitation had been felt in the neighbourhood, this supposition was not generally accepted. The editor of the *Leeds Mercury*, who visited the spot a few days afterwards, described it in that paper as follows:—

"Crow-hill, the scene of this phenomenon, is about seven miles from Keighley and six from Colne, at an elevation of about 1,000 feet above the former place. The top of the moor, which is nearly level, is covered with peat and other accumulations of decayed vegetables of a less firm texture; the whole appeared saturated with water, and in most places trembled under the tread of the foot. The superfluous water at the east end of the moor, drained into small rivulets at the bottom of a deep glen or gill down a precipitous range of rocks which presented the appearance of a gigantic staircase. This rivulet passes down the valley to Keighley, and enters the Aire near

Stockbridge, about a mile below that town. At the distance of about 500 yards from the top of the glen the principal discharge seems to have taken place. Here a very large area of about 1200 yards in circumference is excavated to the depth of from four to six yards, and at a short distance from this chasm there is a similar excavation, but much less in extent. The concavities have been emptied not only of their water, but also of their solid contents. A channel, of about twelve yards in width and seven or eight in depth has been formed quite to the mouth of the gill, down which a most amazing quantity of water was precipitated with a violence and noise of which it is difficult to form an adequate conception, and which was heard to a considerable distance. Stones of an immense size and weight were hurried by the torrent more than a mile. It is impossible to form any computation of the quantity of earthy matter which has been carried down into the valley, but that it was enormous is evident from the vast quantities deposited by the torrent in every part of its course, and from the great quantity which our river still contains. This destructive torrent was confined within narrow bounds by the high glen through which it passed, until it reached the hamlet of Ponden, where it expanded over some corn-fields, covering them to the depth of several feet; it also filled up the mill-pond, choking up the watercourse, and thereby putting an entire stop to the works. A stone bridge was also nearly swept away at this place, and several other bridges in its course were materially damaged. We feel happy, however, in being able to state that it was not fatal to life in a single instance. The torrent was seen coming down the glen before it reached the hamlet by a person who gave the alarm, and thereby saved the lives of several children who would otherwise have been swept away. The torrent at this time presented a breast of seven feet high. The track and extent of this inundation of mud may be accurately traced all the way from the summit of the hill to the confluence of the rivulet with the Aire, by the black deposit which is left on its banks. The first bursting of the bog took place at six o'clock in the evening of Thursday the 2nd inst., and another very considerable discharge occurred on the following day about eight o'clock in the morning, and it is highly probable that other extensive portions of the bog will from time to time hereafter be discharged into the Aire in a similar manner. No human being was on the spot to witness the commencement of this awful phenomenon, and of course we cannot arrive at an absolute degree of certainty as to its cause: the most probable one is the bursting of a waterspout. The suddenness and violence of the disruption strongly favour this supposition. It would evidently require a power acting with a great degree of momentum to move and break in pieces the large and almost solid masses of peat and turf which were forced down the hill, to say nothing of the detached rocks which were moved. The state of the atmosphere about the time when the disruption took place also renders this solution highly probable, the air being fully charged with electric matter. 'At the time of the eruption,' says Mr. Bronte, 'the clouds were copper-coloured, gloomy and lowering, the atmosphere was strongly electrified, and unusually close. These appearances, as they indicated, were followed by a severe thunder-storm, during which it is more than probable that some heavily-loaded cloud poured its contents upon the spot.' We may add, in support of this hypothesis, that more water seems to have been sent down the glen than could have been supplied by the contents of the two bogs which have been excavated. But perhaps a still more important inquiry is, what can be done to prevent a recurrence of similar eruptions? This is rather a difficult question. There is, however, no doubt but the drainage of the moss would remove the danger, as no instance exists of either the bursting or floating away of a drained bog. Probably the channels now made, should they remain open, will give the required stability to the peaty soil."

With all deference to the opinions of the Rev. P. Bronte and Mr. E. Baines, we think that the cause of the disruption is to be ascribed neither to an earthquake nor a waterspout, but simply to the pressure of the accumulated and pent-up waters having become too great for the stability of their mossy embankment.

The scene of this geological movement is situated at the western extremity of the great basin of the Humber, where a portion of each descending shower falling on the summit finds its way into that river and thence into the German Ocean, whilst the other portion is as faithfully delivered by the Ribble into the Irish Sea. This place, according to the statement of Mr. Mitchell, author of the "Dendrologia," is 998 feet above the level of Keighley, and the parish church at Keighley being 366 feet above the sea-level, its entire altitude must be 1,364 feet.

Keighley National Schools were built in 1825, at the cost of £1,750.; they are at present attended by about 334 boys, 239 girls, and 110 infants.

A branch-office of the Craven Bank was established here in 1834.

March 16th, 1847, the Leeds and Bradford extension line of Railway was opened to Keighley, and in 1849 joined to the East Lancashire at Colne, from whence it proceeds to Manchester, Liverpool, and various other parts of Lancashire.

1849. As we deem it an honour to the town, we cannot deny ourselves the pleasure of recording the fact that John Milligan, Esq., Surgeon, Keighley, M.R.C.S., L.S.A., and Hon. Cor. Fel. Med. Soc., London, excited considerable surprise among the medical profession in the metropolis by carrying off the Fothergillian Gold Medal of this year. The subject of the prize essay was "On the Influence of Civilization upon Health and Disease."

In the early part of 1853 Keighley was made a Petty Sessional Division of the West-Riding, and a Superintending Constable was appointed. In the following year a new Court House, Prison and Constable's Residence were erected.

Keighley a Post Town. Some time ago a memorial was forwarded from Keighley to the post-office authorities complaining of their postal arrangements, and praying for the privileges of a post town. We are happy to say that their prayer was granted; and the first bag was made up for Keighley in London in the first week of February, 1854. Great inconvenience was previously experienced by the letters having to be sorted in Leeds: this of course is now done away with.

A Board of Health was constituted Sept. 20th, 1855, and its benefits are already to be seen in every part of the town, though a few owners of house property, out of whose pockets a goodly portion of the needful comes, think they pay too dearly for their whistle.

The West-Riding Constabulary Force was constituted on the 1st of January, 1857. The Keighley Petty Sessional Division includes the parishes of Keighley and Bingley, the townships of Haworth, Wilsden, and Steeton-with-Eastburn; its official staff consists of one superintendent, one inspector, two sergeants, and twenty police constables.

A beautiful Cemetery, situate at Utley, has just been completed, at an expense of near £6000. of borrowed money. One part of the ground is apportioned to the Establishment, another part to the Dissenters. The former was consecrated on Friday, March 27th, 1857, by the Right Rev. Robert Bickersteth, D.D., the Lord Bishop of Ripon, who afterwards gave an affecting address in the open air to the assembled multitude; the latter was formally opened by the Dissenters on the following Wednesday. A third portion is unappropriated, being reserved for the use of the party that may first need it.

VILLAGES AND OTHER OBJECTS IN THE NEIGHBOURHOOD.

We now propose taking a hasty sketch, not only of the villages in this parish, but of the adjoining places of Riddlesden, Marley, and Hainworth, in the parish of Bingley, with such other objects in the neighbourhood as may be deemed worthy of notice, prefacing our intended topographical sketch by a few remarks on the supposed origin of the two parishes. Keighley, Bingley and Haworth, though not the offspring of one parent, may be considered children of the same age. The principal part of Keighley, and probably the township of Morton, sprung from Kildwick, the yet extensive and nearest Domesday parish; Morton till the latter part of the seventeenth century having continued a part of the Skipton Fee, owing suit and service to the Court Leet of that place; and itwas most likely on this account that Bingley Parish, which is in the civil jurisdiction of Skyrack, was comprehended in the deanery of Craven. Probably the main part of Bingley and the small portion of this parish contained in the Skyrack division were taken, as Bradford and Halifax are known to have been, from the once extensive parish of Dewsbury. Haworth township, or, as it is more frequently called, Haworth parish, which we suppose to be co-eval in date, will be found nearly of the same extent as the two adjoining parishes. Keighley parish has been found to contain 10,160 acres; Haworth township, 10,540; and Bingley, without Morton township, 9,890, with Morton, which some suppose to have been added at a later period, 13,180. The three parishes, without Morton, may have been estimated at 10,000 acres each, more or less, which leads to the supposition that they were surveyed and set out at the same time. In support of this idea, we may state that the three churches are first mentioned at periods not widely varying from each other.

It is stated in an extract in the "History of Bradford" from Hopkinson's MS., that in the 43rd of Elizabeth, the two parishes of Keighley and Bingley were assessed by an equal rate, at eightpence each per week; and "at Leeds Sessions, the 13th day of April, in the 44th of Elizabeth, before Sir John

Saville, Thomas Fairfax and other Justices, it was agreed that they should meet at Wakefield upon Wednesday in next Whitsuntide week, touching soldiers' pensions, assessments and other matters, and then agree upon a particular estreat and perfect assessment of the towns within the wapontakes, to be and remain a precedent to direct other justices to make an equal assessment for these parts when occasion should require." In this adjustment, which we may suppose would give a correct view of the relative wealth and importance of the several places mentioned therein, Haworth is assessed at twelve-pence and Bingley at nine-pence. Though Keighley is not mentioned in the latter citation, we may suppose that it would be equal to Bingley, as in the preceding year. If so, Haworth in the year 1602 exceeded Keighley or Bingley, either in opulence, or the number of its inhabitants, or in both, by one-fourth. Did not our limits forbid it, we would indulge our pleasure by including a description of Haworth, a place noted as the residence of the reverend and apostolic Wm. Grimshaw, and still more so as that of the amiable and distinguished novelist, the late Miss Bronte, whose fame draws pilgrims to her shrine from all parts of the country.

THE HITCHING STONE.

On the confines of Keighley Common, at an elevation of 1,200 feet, and upwards of five miles from the town, stands an isolated and ponderous mass of coarse grit, called the 'Hitching Stone,' said to have been hitched or thrown over the valley by an old woman from the top of Rumbles Moor! It is a well-known place of rendezvous for the numerous parties of gentlemen and others who resort to the moor for the purpose of grouse shooting, and who on the afternoon of the twelfth of August have frequently races and other diversions to finish their day's sport. It is thought by some to have been connected with the worship of the Druids; but probably it will be considered most interesting in a geological point of view. A hole running through its whole length, perhaps 24 feet, is evidently the mould or matrix of an enormous fish. The stone is what geologists term 'millstone grit,' occupying in the earth's crust an intermediate position between the carboniferous limestone and the valuable coal measures.

Near the west corner of the stone may be observed a niche or recess, called the 'Priest's Chair,' communicating with the before-named hole, where several persons may sit concealed free from the wind and rain on all sides but the west. As regards this place it is probable that advantage was taken of a rare natural phenomenon in order to connect it with the gloomy superstition and gross idolatry of a dark and remote age.

At a short distance are two smaller stones, the one on the east called 'Kidstone,' the other 'Navaxstone,' which stands at the terminus of the race-course. In the absence of any certainty of the meaning of *Navax*, may we not reasonably suppose it to be a corruption of *Navarch*, commander of a fleet, and metonymically misapplied to this stone by some pedantic sportsman who retained but faint traces of his school-Greek? 'Navarch's stone' would, on the tongue of the country-folks, easily glide into 'Navaxstone.'

SLITHERYFORE.

This place consists of a number of farm-houses pleasantly situated at the source of the North Beck amid the forkings of the stream, from one of which crossing the road at the bottom of a steep hill, it is supposed to have taken its name—Slitheryfore meaning, as some would intimate, the ford of the slippery hill.

Dr. Whitaker, whose supercilious contempt of manufactures is well known, laments the change that had recently come over this parish in the following eloquent and pathetic terms:—" Before the introduction of manufactures, the parish of Keighley did not want its retired glens and well-wooded hills; but the clear mountain torrent is now defiled; its scaly inhabitants suffocated by filth; its murmurs lost in the din of machinery; and the native music in its overhanging groves exchanged for oaths and curses." But however guilty the rest of the parish may be, Slitheryfore at least must stand acquitted of the odious charge; for here the air is still pure, and the water uncontaminated; the limpid brook still murmurs at the bottom of the deep glen, and each returning season is still hailed by the free and uninterrupted harmony of its native choir.

NEWSHOLME.

Of the several villages in the parish of Keighley, Newsholme occupies the most elevated ground, standing on a fine dry hill between the main stream of the North Beck and another brook which passes Newsholme, and joins the former at Goose-eye a short distance below. We are informed in the Domesday Survey that in the "Berewick of Newhuse, William had one carucate of land to be taxed." It is probable that this village took its name from the circumstance of a conspicuous farm-house having been built on the top of the hill, and called by way of distinction, the 'Newhouse;' in the course of time, other houses having sprung up around, it began to assume the form of a village, and was called 'Newhouseham,' which would be easily contracted to Newsholme. A large and most excellent building was erected here by R. & S. Hall, in the year 1670, one part of which was lately made into a place of worship, and licensed for the service of the Church of England. A Day-school was also established under the patronage of the late John Greenwood Esq. of Knoll, the principal proprietor of the village. Here are two small mills, but on account of their contracted size and distance from the town there is scarcely any work done at them, except a little wood-turning.

Newsholme-dean is a deep and pleasant valley, more frequently spoken of than seen. Its few inhabitants still retain those simple and artless habits which make the lover of nature "think it a happy life to be no better than a homely swain." They have a saying which would puzzle a critic to tell to what part of speech it belongs. When any of the rustics meets with an unexpected difficulty in his work, he, nothing daunted, and with the utmost good humour, exclaims, "Well, there wor ollos a hill agean a slack, an' two i' Newsholme-dein!"

HOLM-HOUSE.

Happily it requires no great share of etymological skill to be able to determine with some degree of plausibility the origin of the names of many of our villages. The true meaning of Holm-house cannot be mistaken. We find the holm, for the most part, lying "contiguous to a running stream," and formed of the alluvial deposit brought from the higher ground by the mechanical force of the water. Here is a small worsted mill, and at Slack-lane, a little to the south-west, a Baptist chapel and burial-ground.

GOOSE-EYE.

The name of this place, metamorphosed by a singular process of rustic refinement to the eye of a goose, when restored to its original form and meaning will be 'Goose-hee,' now properly 'Goose-high' or 'height;' the affix, *hee*, being one of the many terms used in our northern dialect to designate a hill or elevated ground, as illustrated in the old song of the battle of Otterburn.

> "The roe full reckless there she runs
> To make thee game and glee,
> The falcon and the pheasant both
> Among the holts on hee."

We anticipate the objection that the village is in a deep vale by remarking that it is high with respect to Keighley, and as higher ground must be climbed to reach it, the name may have been at first applied in view of this fact.

In or near this place there are two worsted mills, and an extensive paper manufactory. The main stream of the North Beck issuing out of Newsholmedean is met here by another brook from Holm-house, and from the almost contiguous village on its northern bank the united stream, if we are rightly informed by Harrison, an old historian, receives the name of Laycock.

LAYCOCK.

LAYCOCK, which was formerly spelled and is still pronounced 'Lacok,' appears to have originally meant 'little lake;' the holme, as may be supposed, at the beck side having been the site of a small lake or standing pool; the termination *ock* being formerly used as a diminutive, as may be seen in the words *hillock, bullock, paddock, parrock,* &c. In William the Conqueror's time, "Ravensuar had two carucates of land to be taxed in the manor of Lacoc." But it is clear that Laycock soon ceased to exist as a separate manor; and it is highly probable that Keighley, Laycock, and the subordinate hamlets of Newsholme and Braithwaite, had become one consolidated lordship long before the grant of Free Warren to Henry Kighley. At all events there were only four lords returned for the five manors in the year 1316, and as Oakworth is known to have existed from the Domesday Survey to the present time it is not unreasonable to suppose that John de Vaux was meant as lord of that place and not Laycock, the latter being then represented by the lord of the manor of Keighley. This village was formerly considered next in degree to Keighley, and it still belongs to a number of wealthy freeholders.

Until lately, the rural sport of dancing round the May-pole was continued here.

242 years before Christ, Lady Flora bequeathed her fortune to the citizens of Rome to celebrate her memory by May-day sports and revelries; the Romans in return evinced their gratitude by exalting her among their 30,000 deities, as the goddess of flowers, fruits, and herbs. The festival soon spread over western Europe, and engrafted itself in the affections of the people by giving them an opportunity of expressing their joy and hilarity at the commencement of a season when Nature unfolds her beauties, dispenses her bounties, and wafts her spicy gales to exhilarate man and enliven the scenes around him. Great excesses having become rather the rule than the exception at these Floralian festivities, our puritan forefathers, not distinguishing between their use and abuse, and forgetful of their boyhood, hurled their anathemas at the innocent and athletic diversions as well as profanities of sweet May-day, whence they gradually declined, and they are now almost extinct.

> "Those healthful sports that grac'd the peaceful scene,
> Lived in each look and brightened all the green;
> These, far departing, seek a kinder shore,
> And rural mirth and manners are no more."

In this place there is a neat and commodious Methodist Chapel and Sunday School. The north side of the parish, now a church district, (entitled the "Keighley North District") is under the pastoral care of the Rev. Henry Taylor, and he or his successor will continue the services at Newsholme till the erection of the intended new church, which will probably stand somewhere in the vicinity of Laycock.

In this neighbourhood, at a farm house called Whorls, breathed, slept, and died, William Sharp, alias 'Old Three-laps,' who went to bed in the year 1807, and lay there in the enjoyment of good health till 1856, a period of 49 years! He was the son of a farmer in good circumstances, and from an early age showed singular habits of character, frequently ranging the adjoining moors with his gun, and spending whole nights alone in the open air. At the age of 30 he obtained the consent of a young woman to become united to him in wedlock. The wedding-day was fixed, on the morning of which Sharp, in company with a friend, wended his way down to the parish church, and there in anxious suspense waited for the arrival of the bride elect, but the father of the damsel disapproving of the match, kept her confined at home. This great slip between the cup and the lip preyed heavily on the susceptible mind of the ardent lover. He returned home, consigned himself to a small room measuring about nine feet each way, with the determination to spend the rest of his existence between the blankets; and the infatuated man kept his resolution to the last. The floor of this room was covered with stone flags; in one corner was a fireplace which could only be used when the wind blew from one or two points of the compass; the window was well fastened down, and where some of the squares had been broken, was carefully patched up with wood. At the time of his death this window had not been opened for 38 years! The furniture comprised an old oak clock, minus weights and pendulum, almost covered with a thick net-work of cobwebs, a small round table of dark oak, and a plain, unvarnished, four-post bed, without hangings. In this dreary cell, whose only inlet for fresh air during 38 years was the doorway, occasionally left open, did this strange being immure himself. He obstinately refused to speak to any one, and if spoken to, never answered even those who were his constant attendants. His father, by will, made provision for his temporal wants, and he seemed unconscious of any other. He ate his meals latterly in a curious way, for in process of time his legs became contracted and drawn up towards his body, and when about to eat his food he used to roll himself over, and so take his meals in a kneeling posture, and to prevent any crumbs from getting into the blanket on which he lay, he turned the under blanket over and eat them off the bed-tick. In a physical point of view he did great credit to his food, for his flesh was firm, fair, and unwrinkled, save with fat, and the estimate of his weight was about 240 pounds. During the whole period of this self-imposed confinement he never had any serious illness till the last week of his life, when his appetite failed, and his limbs became partially benumbed, and death terminated his morbid existence on Monday, the 3rd of March, 1856. Just before he expired he was heard to exclaim "Poor Bill, poor Bill, poor Bill Sharp!" the most connected sentence he had been known to utter for many years. As might be expected, the curious came far and wide to see this eccentric person, and whenever a stranger was ushered into his den, he immediately buried his head in the bed-clothes, and on one occasion he contrived to make a hole in the bed-tick and hide himself among the feathers. Thousands assembled in Keighley church and grave-yard, where he was buried, to pay their last tribute of wonder at his obsequies. The coffin excited much attention from its extraordinary size, being more like a great oak chest than a coffin; it was two feet four inches in depth, and so heavy that it required eight men with strong ropes to lower it into the grave. The weight of the coffin and its contents was estimated at 480 lbs.

BRAITHWAITE.

THIS place, which is about half-a-mile nearer to the town than Laycock, is supposed to have been originally a wood on the brae or brow of the hill, and Braithwaite-edge its boundary. The *thwaite*, as understood by Thoresby, "was land severed from a wood, grubbed up and made arable, which gave name in this district to many places." It was probably a dependent hamlet of the ancient manor of Laycock, the latter place being still allowed a kind of precedence. Much of the land about this village was, prior to the date of the Inclosure Act, a wild and open common; but what was lately a part of the Keighley Moor— a bleak and sterile waste—is now cultivated land, affording corn and milk to the industrious community of the village.

Mr. Abraham Shackleton, an inhabitant of this place, who began to keep an account of the births, deaths, and number of individuals living at the close of each year in 1791, and ending 1846, found that whilst only 1 in 50 died annually out of the mixed population of this elevated spot, the average of life fell something short of 21 years, the number of inhabitants at the commencement of this account being 34, at its close, 100; the total number of births 184, total of deaths

76, one-third of which appear to have died in their first year.

From the accumulated observations of the above-named gentleman, who died March 25th, 1857, after spending a life protracted to eighty years in the delightful alternations of light labour in his garden and extensive reading in general literature and natural history, we have derived the following invaluable meteorological results. We deem these results to be of such importance to health, scientific agriculture, and indirectly to trade, that we have made some comparisons between them and those in other parts of Yorkshire, and we find that in many instances the balance is in favour of our own locality. It has been remarked that this county possesses peculiarities of climate due to the remarkable mould in which its masses of land are cast. On occasions of epidemics these peculiarities appear to have a distinguishable influence on their distribution, as we have often noticed in the case of typhus fever. The editor lately occupied a cottage at Oakworth, where the first victim fell to this disease many years ago, and the infectious destroyer has at intervals continued to ravage the neighbourhood until now; though, happily, its recent outbreaks have assumed a milder form. The character of this disease is perhaps not so much due to the nature of the soil as some other complaints, yet the climate and soil together do, to a certain extent, produce a marked influence over it. Hence it is needful for persons of delicate habit, who wish to preserve their health and have the power to select their place of abode, to pay particular regard to the following and kindred data.

A Fahrenheit's thermometer, suspended in a chamber where no fire was kept, from 1800 to 1854 inclusive, gave these results—

	DEGREES.
Average annual temperature	49.58
The hottest years were 1826 and 1831, they each gave the same average measure, viz.	53.25
The coldest year, 1800, gave only	46.00
The 16th of January was the coldest day of the year, its average measure was	36.85
The 30th of July the hottest, it indicated	63.66

Annual temperature at York, 48°.2; Halifax, 48°.3; Malton, 47°.65.

The greatest yearly average height of the barometer from 1825 to 1855 was 30.22 inches, in 1825; the least, 27.25 inches, in 1843; the mean average for the period, 29.116 inches.

The greatest number of rainy days in any one year from 1798 to 1855 was 296, in 1830; the least, 219, in 1855; the yearly average for the whole 58 years, 252.9 days.

The maximum depth of rain falling in any one year from 1839 to 1856 was 45.37 inches, in the year 1852; the minimum, 20.83 inches, in the year 1855; the average yearly fall throughout the entire 18 years was 32.703 inches. The yearly average at York is 24 inches; Scarborough, 23; Halifax, 33; Settle, 43; Bolton by Bolland, 47; and Keyingham, 18 inches.

The most prevalent winds are from the west; the next are those from the south-west and north-west, which are about equal; the least frequent are from the direct south and east, which are nearly equal; the north-east wind, so dreadful to invalids, is common in the spring season.

These observations were always taken at 8 o'clock in the morning, at a house situated 774 feet above the sea-level, and 408 feet above the town, and on the side of a hill with a southern aspect, and whose ridge, running east and west, rises 231 feet higher than the house.

FELL LANE.

FELL LANE stands on the south side of the stream and still somewhat nearer to the town. We are not aware that the word *fell* was ever used in this locality, as in some of the more northern counties, to denote a hill or mountain. Had this been the case it would be of no avail in this particular instance in directing us to the origin of the name, for we are convinced that this place was so called from a family of that name. On reference to the parish register it will be found that in the year 1628 Ellen Fell was married to Edward Beanlands, and there are a few old persons still living who can remember a 'Maister and Dame Bellands' (Mr. and Mrs. Beanlands) living there, and employing the main part of the inhabitants of the village in the combing, spinning, and dyeing of stocking worsted. On the first appearance of Goldsmith's "Deserted Village," it was objected that the depopulation it deplored was nowhere to be seen, and the disorders it lamented were only to be found in the Poet's own imagination; but the poem, which appears to have been too truly prophetic, is now sadly and lamentably verified in many of our villages; for in the midst of a vastly increasing population, there are places beyond the reach and influence of the mills, perhaps once the healthiest and happiest spots in the land, which now present the gloomy appearance of depopulation and decay. Fell Lane, though within a mile of the town, with two mills in its vicinity, was unhappily thrown into this situation by the sudden death of a spirited manufacturer.

It affords us much pleasure to record that this place has been lately touched by the wand of the capitalist, and its name erased from the list of our deserted villages. The mills have been supplied with machinery; a number of new cottages has been erected; and it is to be hoped that the village will in future share only in such changes and fluctuations as are common to the trade of the district.

JENNET'S WELL.

Before leaving the north side of the parish it may be advisable to notice 'Jennet's Well,' long an object of local attachment and religious veneration. It was situated at Black Hill, and is now one of the main feeders of the Calversyke-hill reservoir. Janet appears to have been the tutelary saint of Keighley and the neighbourhood: the old boys protesting and the young ones asseverating 'By Jen!' It will likewise be found to have been a name of great repute in the early part of the parish register, and it still lingers (though considered an old-fashioned name) in the remoter parts of the parish.

Westward of Jennet's Well there was another fountain, emphatically styled the 'true well,' and probably from its once boasted efficacy intended as a rival to the former. This spring though no longer remembered for its healing qualities, evidently gave name to the farmhouse denominated 'True Well Hole.'

THE SOUTH-WEST OR SUN-SIDE OF THE PARISH.

We have taken the liberty of stepping a little beyond the limits of our own parish in this direction, in order to make Camel Cross the starting point of our pedestrian tour. Camel is no doubt a corruption of Gamel, the name of a considerable Saxon proprietor of the land in these parts, who set up this cross near the highway side, probably for the two-fold purpose of determining the extent of his boundaries and reminding the devout traveller of his Christian duties. According to the Domesday account, Gamel had in the time of William the Conqueror, fifteen carucates of land in the manor of Bradford, ten in Carlton and Lothersdale, and three in the manor of Glusburn and Malsis, amounting in the whole to near three thousand acres.

Not far from Camel Cross is a place called the Wool or Wolf Stones; but Two Laws is generally considered the farthest extremity of the parish, being six miles from the town. It was probably called Two Laws from its situation on the borders of the two counties, or, as some antiquarians might suggest, from the two hills, *law* being an old word for hill. The inhabitants of the 'Sun Side' of the parish are partly distributed on the banks of the 'Sun Beck,' in small villages clustering about the several mills of the valley, but more generally in rows and groups of houses at irregular distances on the line of road leading to the town.

Scartop is the highest place in the course of the stream. Here is a small Methodist Chapel, and at Oldfield, a little below, a chapel belonging to the Primitive Methodists. It appears that Oldfield formerly belonged to the ancient family of Pighills, but was subsequently the residence of a somewhat conspicuous family of the name of Midgley, lords of the manor of Haworth, who alienated that lordship to the Ferrands. Oldfield House was also the residence of that eccentric individual, Mr. John Mitchell, commonly called 'The Old Gentleman,' who was buried at the bottom of one of his own fields. He was a person of very reserved habits and of a misanthropic turn of mind, the author of several books, and one who like Akenside's Virtuoso,

> "Could tell e'en if a mite were lean or fat,
> And read a lecture o'er the entrails of a gnat."

We now arrive at Harehill Free School, which stands within a small croft on the skirts of Oakworth Moor. This school was founded by Sarah Heaton, 1743, she having left the sum of £200. for that purpose. This, with an additional sum (borrowed), was laid out in the purchase of a farm at Whitehill, which, under careful and judicious management, together with the house and croft, is said to be now worth £40. a year. A neat building has been lately erected on the site of an old one, and fit up with all the accommodations of a country school. The first trustees of this school appear to have been Nathan Pighills, Robert Sugden and William Midgley. The trustees in 1846 were Joseph Greenwood, Esq. of Springhead, Mr. John Wright of Oldfield, and Mr. Abm. Wright of Westhouse. Mr. Thomas S. Wright is the schoolmaster.

Having passed Pighill's Hill, or, as it is now spelled, 'Pickles Hill,' where is another small chapel, we approach an old house called 'Laverock Hall.'

LAVEROCK HALL. 143

Some philologists derive Laverock from the Chaldee; this is rather far-fetched, and quite unnecessary for our purpose, as it is a common name for *lark* in Scotland.

> "The lav'rock shuns the palace gay,
> And o'er the cottage sings;
> For nature smiles as sweet, I ween,
> To shepherds as to kings."

What was once a genteel edifice, in the Elizabethan style of architecture, erected in the year 1641 by Henry and Mary Pighills, is now used as a common farm-house. In this family we meet with a curious illustration of the origin and application of names. From certain hills, perhaps long the favourite resort of a well-known family of quadrupeds, the biped owner of the soil acquired the redoubtable surname, 'de Pighills.' In the course of succeeding generations the compliment was again returned by the family, and the name of Pighill's Hill conferred on a part of the road and a number of houses not far from the ancient dwelling. The above-named Henry, who died, 1647, was succeeded at Laverock Hall by his third son, Nathan Pighills, who dying unmarried at an advanced age, left Laverock Hall, Carr Head, and the bulk of his property to John Bradley, the son of his niece. Mr. N. Pighills had a sister Mary, who married Mr. Edmund Laycock of Cowling, whose only surviving daughter married Mr. Thomas Bradley of Cononley. Their son, John Bradley, born 1682, becoming the especial favourite and eventually heir of his great-uncle as above stated, married the daughter of Mr. John Green of Southwark, Merchant, and had a son John, who died without issue. He had likewise a daughter

Elizabeth, who in 1740 married Mr. Richard Wainman, ancestor of William B. Wainman, Esq., the present owner of Laverock Hall and the more eligible modern mansion and estate of Carr Head. In ·1707 we find Mr. Nathan Pighills, in company with the Rev. Miles Gale, Rector of Keighley, and Mr. Charles Townley, brother of Richard Townley, Esq. of Townley Hall, paying a visit to Mr. Giles, the eminent glass painter in York.* After the death of Mr. Nathan Pighills, which took place in 1712, the family began to decline in the parish of Keighley, though somewhat plentiful in the neighbouring townships, intelligent members of which are now strangely acknowledging as substitutes for their original surname the corrupt and derisive epithets, Pighells, Pigheels, and Pickles. The Laverock Hall estate was purchased by Thomas Pighills of Royd House, in the parish of Keighley, in the year 1585, of Thomas Lockwood of Lynthwaite, who obtained it by marriage with Mary, the heiress of W. Sattonstall. It was previously held by the Stansfields, and may be traced back, as we are credibly informed, from deeds in the possession of its present owner to Richard de Haworth, 1320.

A little to the south is a farm-house called 'Street Head, which is supposed to derive its name from its situation on the Roman way or street running from a point of the Ilkley and Manchester road near Castlestead-ring, to Colne. The name of the neighbouring village of Stanbury, or stone fort, favours this supposition.

Next in point of time to this ancient site is a group of farm-houses and cottages on the east, bearing the

---

* "Thoresby's Correspondence," page 78, vol. II.

significant name of 'Scholes,' from *schales, skales,* or *shiels,* a term applied in Saxon times to tents or cottages erected for those who attended upon cattle.

OAKWORTH.

OAKWORTH, once the head, and as it may be supposed, the principal village in the lordship, now consists of a few dwellings unworthy of any particular notice. The historian of Halifax, speaking of Holdsworth, says, "the word *worth* sometimes signifies a farm or possession, sometimes a court or place, and in a military sense, a fort: the other part of the word, *oak,* plainly intimates that the oak once flourished here. The manor of Oakworth was given by the Conqueror to Gilbert Tyson, and in the year 1316 it belonged to John de Vaux. It was afterwards held by the ancient family of Copley of Batley and Oxenhope, along with Sutton and Cowling, in allusion to which we cannot resist the temptation of introducing from Scatchard's "History of Morley," the following picture of the so much envied 'good old times.'—" Sir Bryan Thornhill of Thornhill, by deed dated, Batley, 1334, gave leave to Adam de Oxenhope to assign over to William de Carlinghow, the Chaplain, one messuage, two bovates of land,* and thirty shillings rent, which the said Adam held of the said Bryan as parcel of the manor of Batley, and in consequence, and with the leave of the King and of William Melton, Archbishop of York, the said Adam founded the chantry in Batley church for his soul and the souls of Margery his wife, Robert his father, Maud his mother, William de Cop-

---

* A bovate, oxgang, or ox-gate, was as much land as an ox could plough in a year, and it varied from 8 to 28 acres.

ley; John, William, Thomas and Bryan his sons, Thomas de Thornton and Ellen his wife, and John de Manningham, for all whose goods he had illgotten, and for all the faithful departed." The author observes:—"Many of the great people in Edward the Third's reign continued to be robbers and assassins, and these were the ways by which they were taught to quiet their consciences, especially in sickness." From this extract the thoughtful reader will see the folly of wishing for a return of the falsely called 'good old times,' when our ancestors had such an easy method of appeasing conscience, sanctifying pelf, bribing the Judge of the quick and the dead, and purchasing heaven.

Alvery Copley, who died 1598, was "seized of Batley, Sutton, and Oakworth;" but soon after his time, as we are given to understand, the thirty-two tenants or freeholders of this liberty were by a deed now in the possession of Mr. William B. Wainman of Carr Head, not only freed from the ancient customary services, but constituted joint lords of the manor, they being now entitled to the mineral and manorial rights in common with the chief lord; and as an equivalent or proper compensation for so valuable a privilege, the emancipated tenants agreed to pay a certain annual sum, called a 'free-rent.' In the time of Mr. Gale, the chief lord of Oakworth liberty was Mr. Michael Stell of Well Head, in this parish, whose son Michael, subsequent to the year 1733, sold it to the Ferrands, and the free-rent is now collected by the tenant of Goodley Farm for William Busfeild Ferrand, Esq., Harden Grange, son of the late Currer Busfeild, Esq., who has assumed the patronymic of his grandfather since succeeding to his estates.

LANE-ENDS—OAKWORTH HALL.

The two most central and populous places on this side of the parish are Lane-ends, and Oakworth Hall. They lie almost contiguous, and form together a kind of metropolis for Oakworth liberty, which in 1844 was made a parochial district, when the Rev. James Chesterton Bradley, M.A., was preferred by the Ecclesiastical Commissioners to the newly-formed Incumbency. The National School was opened in February, 1845, and was at one time attended by more than 200 scholars, but a pressure of commercial calamities having caused Mr. James Mitchell, the chief supporter of Lane ends, to stop a part of his machinery, many families have left the place, and the number of scholars is now much diminished. The new church, denominated Christ Church, was erected in 1846; Mr. Wallen of Huddersfield was the architect, and the ground for the church and church-yard the liberal gift of the lady of the manor, the late Mrs. S. Ferrand of St. Ives. The cost of the church, including £150. invested in the 3 per cent. Consols for repairs, was about £2,000. All the sittings are free. The living is a perpetual curacy, valued at £150. a year, in the alternate patronage of the Crown and the Bishop of Ripon. The Rev. John Smith, B.A., is the present incumbent. In 1856, a handsome parsonage, in the Elizabethan style, was erected at Sykes Head. Near the two places there are several worsted mills. The Wesleyans have a large and beautiful chapel at Oakworth Hall, and the Primitive Methodists a small one at Lane-ends. The particular building, entitled 'Oakworth Hall,' which appears to have given name to the place, presents a somewhat genteel appearance, and was erected in the year 1702 by W. C. (William Clough). On a stone in the back part of the house there is to be seen a small figure of a man on horseback, with three goats trippant, but not on a coat or shield. In 1851, Oakworth Ecclesiastical District was found to contain 2,686 inhabitants.

On the Parish Feast Monday there were within the writer's recollection horse races on the adjoining moor. Foot races, quoit playing, pitch and toss, knacks, leaping, and wrestling, &c., are still the out-door festal amusements of the young folks of this place; and when darkness sets in, the jolly blades of the rustic crew resort to the public-house, where they drink and smoke, sing and dance, and not unfrequently squabble and fight, till next morning. It is a pleasing sign of the progress of education and morality in this locality that the riotous scenes of former times are now rarely enacted; and the diminishing number of those who still sacrifice at the shrine of Bacchus, and seek for pleasure in wantonness and profanity, leads us to hope that innocent recreations mingled with "the feast of reason and the flow of soul," will ere long supplant all other means of pastime and holiday enjoyments. The Keighley Parish Feast, or Rush Bearing, is held on the third Sunday after old St. Peter's Day, the wake or feast of the town.

On February 20th, 1781, was born at Lane-ends, Isaac Butterfield, who at the age of twenty months was three feet in height, and weighed nearly eight stones. He was exhibited as a gigantic child, at Spring Gardens, London, where he died, February 1st, 1783.

On the banks of the stream between Lane-ends and the town may be noticed Dockroyd, Cackleshaw, Sykes, Harewood Hill, and Damems, once purely agricultural hamlets, but now strongly imbued with the manufacturing spirit. We suppose Dockroyd to be derived from *dock*, a plant, and *royd*, an essart or ground cleared of wood; Cackleshaw, *cattle shaw*, the word *shaw* or *shay* signifying a woody shade or shelter; Sykes or Syke, boggy brook; and if, as stated by Thoresby, the Saxon word *embe* signifies *circum* in Latin, we have a right to infer that Damems originally meant simply the place or dwellings around the dam.

In the course of the Sun Beck, and within a moderate distance of those places, there are several large worsted mills; but in order to complete our intended survey we must now return to Oakworth Hall, and proceed from thence by the high-road to Keighley. Passing Lidget, or Leodgate, which means road-gate, we arrive at Sykes-head, where there is a considerable building occupied by the Wesleyan Methodists as a Sunday and Day School. It is ornamented in front by a public clock and sun dial, likewise an inscription, stating that "This Sunday School was instituted by William Newsholme, 1784." It was rebuilt by subscription in 1833, and it has a small income derived from the rents of a field and three neighbouring cottages.

At a short distance on the road begins a long row of cottages named Bogthorn, beyond which stands the Poor House, a monument of the wisdom and humanity of the statesmen in the reign of 'good Queen Bess.' This was formerly a school house, as noticed at page 58.

Exleyhead, where a Wesleyan Chapel, which is also used as a Sunday School, has lately been built, is specially to be noticed as the last place in Keighley parish to relinquish the vicious and demoralizing custom of bull-baiting, which, to the credit of public feeling, began to be generally discountenanced about the close of the last century. This revolting sport, as formerly practised here, is thus described:—" On the opening of this sublime amusement (?), the bull is fastened to a stake by a chain which extends to about fifteen yards in length, and terminates in a very strong leather collar passing round his neck, his horns being previously muffled at the points with a composition of tow, tallow, and melted pitch. The attack then commences with dreadful noises of different kinds—bellowings, hootings, huzzaings, and whatever can work the poor animal into a state fury; hats, &c., are aimed at him in front, and he is punctured with sharp-pointed sticks, and irritated with repeated twists of the tail behind. The irritation being judged sufficient, a single bull-dog is first let loose upon the prey, and if he be found incapable of pinning him by the nose to the ground, he is soon assisted by a second, and even by a third; and when these are tired or gored other bull-dogs, howling and impatient of control, are let loose in their turn, till the poor exhausted captive faints beneath the protracted attack, and falls a victim to a sport as barbarous as ever disgraced the race of man." The last of these atrocious scenes originated with a recruiting party of soldiers in the year 1794, who are said to have traversed the country with a bull for the purpose of assembling young men to witness and admire the merry life of a soldier, and entice them to enlistment. At the bull-baiting which took place at Exleyhead on the Tuesday of Parish Feast week, if a number of battles did not succeed the excitement as a natural consequence, it was considered the exalted privilege of the champion of the parish, not to 'throw down the gauntlet,' but to shake the bull-ring by way of defiance. Should the well-known challenge meet with no response, he was considered the belted hero for the ensuing year. The last champion of the bull-ring was a tall, raw-boned figure, known by the appropriate cognomen of 'Will Span.' As an instance of a superstition which still lingers in this parish, it may be mentioned that Will Span was also noted for his supposed power of seeing wraiths or the spectral appearances of persons who are about to die! At the end of the little bridge is a large block of stone like the frustum of an octagonal pyramid with a hole in the middle, which was formerly the crown of a series of sloping circular steps, designated the 'Cross.' It was the pedestal of a stone pillar or cross—it might possibly be that of the May-pole. There is a tradition that the market was held here when the town was infected by the plague of 1645.

After leaving Exleyhead we arrive at 'Haley Croft,' pointed out by tradition as once holy or consecrated ground; but for further information on this dubious subject, we refer the reader to the subjoined extract from a scurrilous poem printed at Halifax, 1817.

> "Their speed soon brought them to the place,
>   Where ancient people say,
> That popish priests did once reside,
>   Read, meditate, and pray.
> Tradition says here stood a church,
>   Which by some magic hands,
> Was in one evening snatch'd from thence,
>   And placed where now it stands."

THWAITES.

According to Thoresby, the word *thwaite* formerly meant a grubbed-up wood; and we may add, that as Mickle-thwaite, the name of a neighbouring village, is always pronounced Mickle-wood, it will be pretty evident that *thwaite* and *wood* are, as used in this locality, nearly synonymous terms. Thwaites was the unnamed manor enumerated in the Domesday Book with Keighley. In 1316 we find it in the posession of John de Thwaites. This family, some time in the latter part of the fifteenth century, became possessed of Denton, in Wharfedale. John, the eminent Lawyer, who, as we have seen it asserted, afterwards became a Judge,* was residing there in 1442, and superintended the Clifford estates during the minority of Lord Thomas. But at that time he was only holding the place in trust; for it appears that "William Brocas, grandson of Agnes Vavasour, made over his estate at Denton, by deed of feofment, to William Gascoigne, John Thwaites, and others, from whom John Vavasour of Weston recovered the same," This noted lawyer, who died 1469, married Isabella, sister of Sir William Ryther, of Harewood Castle, Knight, and was buried by the side of his wife in the chancel of Harewood church. He was uncle by marriage to Sir William Gascoigne, Knight, son of the celebrated judge, who committed Prince Henry, son of Henry IV., to prison for drawing his sword upon him. John Vavasour of Weston and Newton near Ripley, married Elizabeth, daughter of Henry Thwaites, Esq., and made his will, 1482. This family, according to Drake, had a large mansion in the city of York, which descended through the Fairfaxes to the Duke of Buckingham. They held the hereditary office of Larderer of the Kitchen,

---

* In the "Loides and Elmete" he is noticed as "a lawyer of great eminence in Yorkshire."

under our early English kings, whilst residing in that city, for which service they had the manor of Davygate exempt from the jurisdiction of the mayor. Isabel, daughter of John Thwaites, the last male heir of this family, married in the year 1512, William Fairfax, who was High Sheriff of the county of York, in the 26th and 31st of Henry VIII., and who by this marriage acquired the estates of Thwaites, Denton, &c.

The Fairfaxes were raised to the peerage by the title of Baron Fairfax of Cameron, and, as is well known, took a most conspicuous part in the civil wars of the seventeenth century. On turning to "Burke's Peerage," we find that the property of the Fairfaxes in Yorkshire was sold about the year 1739, by Thomas, sixth Baron Fairfax, in order to redeem his manors of Colepepper in the county of Kent. His Lordship was in possession of an immense tract of land in Virginia, and visiting that country about the period above mentioned, he was so captivated with its soil, climate, and beauties, that he resolved to spend the remainder of his days there; and what appears highly singular and worthy of notice, a close union and intimacy seems to have sprung up between the descendants of the English Parliamentary General and the family of George Washington, the great American liberator, both being of Yorkshire origin. "Lawrence Washington, the elder brother of General Washington, married Miss Fairfax, the daughter of his neighbour, William Fairfax, a person of wealth and political station in the colony, and a distant relation of Lord Fairfax, a nobleman of literary tastes and somewhat eccentric habits, who had left England and came to reside in Virginia, where he was proprietor of a vast tract of country lying between the

Potomac and the Rappatiamac rivers, and stretching across the Alleghany Mountains. At the time of George Washington's residence with his brother at Mount Vernon, Lord Fairfax was on a visit to the house of William Fairfax, the father-in-law of Lawrence, and between the two families a constant intercourse was kept up."

A large field at Longlee, belonging to the Ferrands, is still called the Fairfax Copy; and Benjamin Ferrand, Esq., of St. Ives, some eighty years ago, caused a stone pike to be raised as a memorial or token of respect to the memory of that highly distinguished family, which still retains the name of the 'Fairfax Pinnacle.'

Thwaites formerly stood on the right bank and within a field length of the river Aire, but in some wanton freak of the capricious element an entire new channel was excavated, and the hapless village left at a considerable distance. By the younkers of the neighbourhood, Thwaites, Utley, Damems, and Cackleshaw, have been facetiously denominated 'seaports'—this being a regular school-boy's pun. In the time of Gale, "courts either were, or might have been held here;" but this manor, long before Whitaker wrote his "History of Craven," had amalgamated with Keighley, and the inhabitants of the village at the present time only entertain a vague tradition of their former lords and manor-courts. Here, as in most of the other villages, is a small building serving the purposes of a Methodist Chapel and Sunday School; besides which there is a Sunday School or Political Institution belonging to the Chartists.

The ancient family of Thwaites bore, argent, three torteaux in a fess, sable, between three fleurs-de-lis.

UTLEY.

UTLEY, supposed to mean the 'oat' or 'out-field,' is thus briefly noticed in the Domesday Survey:—"Manor in Vtelai, William had one carucate to be taxed." In the year 1316, a Richard de Utley was lord of this place, and the Gilbert Kyghley de Utlay, whose monument still remains in the church, was probably lord of that manor in the latter part of the fourteenth century. Again we find the lordship casually mentioned in the "History of Craven," where, as there stated, it appears to have escheated to the Crown, and was granted by King Henry VIII. to John Carr, Knight. We know no more of this extinct lordship, but suppose it to have been entirely absorbed in the manor of Keighley, anterior to the time of Gale, who does not appear to have known that it ever existed.

It might seem from numerous hillocks of cast earth and other inequalities in some of the fields about this place, that a general search had been made in times past for something valuable. This something so diligently sought after appears to have been limestone pebbles, washed down by floods from the Craven hills at a very remote period; it is a substance long known to the agriculturist and builder as one of primary importance. Prior to the opening of the Leeds and Liverpool Canal, great quantities of the same mineral substance were obtained about Bingley, where the ancient custom of raising it from pits by means of the ladder and the basket, is now but imperfectly remembered.

As a proof of the great antiquity of lime-burning in this district, it may be interesting to state, that whilst proceeding with the line of railway a little below

Bingley, the excavators were much surprised to meet with an old lime-kiln, buried beneath the surface by some sudden, unrecorded, but very extraordinary flood. From the state in which it was found, it was evidently abandoned in consequence of the wreck, and probably whilst the fire was in the kiln. It may likewise be regarded as a curious fact in connection with this subject, that when Skipton Castle, which stands upon limestone rock, was repaired in 1437, the lime used on the occasion had to be sent for to Bolton and Addingham,[*] a distance of six miles, and at a very considerable expense, leaving, as may be observed, the abundant-store from whence it is now derived, to procure a limited supply from the bed of the river Wharfe. It is probable that previous to the invention of gunpowder, now an important agent in blasting, the only rock lime used was such as had been severed in a natural way by frost and other atmospherical agencies during the course of the seasons; and according to a vulgar notion still partially entertained, lime made from the rock is supposed to be unequal in value to that prepared from alluvial or water-borne pebbles.

In this place there is a neat and convenient building belonging to the Independents, serving the purposes of a Chapel and Sunday and Day School; and near to the lower part of the village may be seen the remains of an old bridge over the river Aire, called the 'Jowhole,' which, besides bringing Utley and Holden Park into close contiguity, appears to have connected by means of a very narrow road Keighley with Silsden and Bolton Abbey.

---

[*] See second edition of Whitaker's "History of Craven," page 324.

Elam Grange, on the opposite side of the river, appears to have been the favourite haunt of a fabulous or mythic creation, known to the primitive inhabitants of this part of Airedale as 'Hob of Elam,' alias 'Robin Goodfellow,' and which will be recognised by the readers of Scottish legends as one of the Brownies of North Britain. This mysterious being was a curious compound of clownish stupidity and superhuman celerity, who, whilst treated with kindness and trusted with confidence, was ever ready to lend a helping hand, especially in looking after the sheep and cattle during the night, rescuing the former from the snow-storm and the latter from the sudden summer floods. But apprehending that the latter part of our story may deviate too much from its true northern origin, we shall at once introduce to the notice of the reader the following short but pleasing mythological extract from Phillips's "Rivers, Mountains, and Sea Coast of Yorkshire."—

"Hob was also a familiar and troublesome visitor of one of the farmers, and caused him so much vexation and petty loss that he resolved to quit his house in Farndale, near Kirkby Moor Side, and seek some other home. Very early in the morning as he was trudging on his way, with all his household goods and gods in a cart, he was accosted in good Yorkshire by a restless neighbour, with, 'I see you're flitting.' The reply came from Hob out of the churn,—'Ay, we're flutting;' upon which the farmer concluding that change of air would not rid him of the demon, turned his horse's head homeward. This story is in substance the same as that narrated on the Scottish Border and in Scandinavia, and may serve to show for how long a period and with what conformity, even to the play on the vowel, some traditions may be preserved in secluded districts."

HOLDEN CLIFF AND PARK.

On the skirts of Rumbles Moor, and in the parish of Kildwick may be seen two curious stones, which gave name to the farm-house called 'Doubler-stones,' not as we should suppose from *doubler*, a dish, but from their being first called 'The Double-stones.' They stand almost close together, in the form of two round tables. A little below Doubler-stones, where we meet with a few more stray farm-houses, this wild and remote district assumes the name of Gillgrains, from the grains or forking of the gills, by following any of which we arrive at their junction in Holden* Cliff, a deep, secluded, and romantic glen, rich in natural beauties, and capable of much artificial improvement. On the banks of this cliff may be seen two considerable heaps of scoria or cinders, now covered with greensward, the long-forgotten remains of an iron-furnace or blast. But why, it may be asked, should the blast have been erected here? To be sure there might have been plenty of wood for fuel, and limestone sufficient for the flux, but where was the ironstone to be found? We can only answer by directing the curious reader to the bottom of the cliff, where may be seen the same stratum of iron pyrites which extends over the north-west side of Keighley parish, and now used for repairing the highways. There appear to have been formerly many furnaces or blasts of

---

* Holden, *hol* or *holl*, a deep or narrow vale; *den*, a deep vale, or ravine, or bottom; each syllable being nearly synonymous points out the great depth and abruptness of the place.

this kind in the forest of Knaresborough, as shown by the following interesting paragraph from Thoresby's Diary:—"This forest was once so woody that I have heard of an old writing, said to be reserved in the chest at Knaresborough Church, which obliged them to cut down so much yearly as to make a convenient passage for the wool-carriers from Newcastle to Leeds, &c. Now it is so naked that there is not so much as one left for a way mark, such a consumption did the blasts make, of which I have seen great heaps of slag or cinders overgrown with moss, &c., now often dug up for mending the highways."*

Holden Cliff once served for the northern boundary of a deer park belonging to the Lords Clifford of Skipton Castle, called 'Holden Park.' Holden-gate was perhaps the principal entrance, Pinfold-hill the place where the deer were impounded, and Lodge hill the lodge or homestead of the keeper. Dr. Whitaker says,—"Holden Park was full of aged oaks, and well stocked with deer, which in the minority of the third Earl of Cumberland became the prey of poachers and wood-stealers," and that he had met with no record of the time at which it was disparked; but at page 239 of his "History of Craven," from which these passages are extracted, he informs us that in the year 1654, "the heiresses of the elder and younger line of the Cliffords having succeeded to their respective portions of the family estates, the deer which had hitherto ranged at large over both were now to be appropriated and enclosed." From this transaction, we are enabled to fix the era at which

---

* An intelligent farmer at Harden has just apprised us of the existence of a similar heap of ashes there, and its contents are also used for repairing the roads.

the ancient forests of Craven were finally depopulated of their old and stately inhabitants. In 1846 there still remained one fine old oak flourishing in perfect health and vigour, under whose venerable and far-spreading branches many a lively group of 'dappled deer' in bygone days found shelter. But alas! the sound of the woodman's axe was heard in the distance, and soon a cry went forth that the aged monarch of the park was no more!

Eastward, near Upwood House, the residence of J. A. Busfeild, Esq., and on the line of the Roman road to Ilkley, is the site of a building yclept 'Brass Castle,' and within signal distance of the Roman station at Casty-wood. Mr. Busfeild derives its name from Brae's Castle, or the Castle of the Brae; and he thinks it would be seen from the original Brass Castle at Harden.

RIDDLESDEN HALL.

WE suppose Riddlesden to have taken its name from the red ochreous earth which drains from the clay or coal strata of Morton Banks lodged in some particular holes or hollows, and hence called 'Red Holes Den.' The idea first struck us on seeing some drains of this sort running into the river Aire not far from the old house, though we are aware that *rhydd*, in Celtic, is ford, which seems to point to the river for the etymon. Riddlesden Hall is a large and ancient mansion eligibly situated, and rebuilt or enlarged at various times. The vulgar story, that "Riddlesden Hall was built when meal was a penny a peck," does not carry its origin far enough back, if the time of Edward the First is meant, when meal is said to have been sold at that price. The first authentic account of the place is to be met with in the Domesday Survey, where it is thus noticed:—"Manor in Riddlesden, Ardulf had one carucate to be taxed. Land to one half a plough, value sixteen shillings." The first lord to be met with after the Saxon times appears to have been Simon de Montalt,—living, 1160—younger brother "of Robert de Montalt, Baron de Montalt and Hawarden, in the county of Flint; descended from Eustace de Monte Alto, one of the soldiers of the Conquest," sometimes called the Norman Hunter. "This Simon de Montalt held land in the second fee of Skipton under the De Romilles," and, as stated in the pedigree, was succeeded by his son Richard de Montalt, Lord of Riddlesden, Morton, Potternewton, and Burnby-on-Don, who—his son Simon dying in his lifetime without male issue—gave all his Yorkshire estates to Robert Montalt, son of his cousin Andomer or Aylmer. Andomer, who founded the Yorkshire and only surviving branch of the family, in 1174, accompanying the expedition against William the Lion, had the good fortune to make the Scottish monarch prisoner by surprise, and carrying the royal captive to Henry II., then at Falaise in Normandy, that prince granted to him, instead of his ancient ensigns, a lion, gules, (the lion of Scotland) debruised, two bars, sable, to denote captivity.* From Robert de Montalt, who inherited Riddlesden and the other estates of his cousin Richard, descended Simon de Montalt, whose

* So says the pedigree; but we have a strong suspicion that the symbols depicted on the shield had their origin in the absurd fiction, still lingering in the neighbourhood, which derives Riddlesden from "Red Lion's Den." This question can, however, in no way affect the antiquity and high standing of a family whose name is still to be seen on the rolls of Battle Abbey.

daughter and heiress married Robert Paslew, founder of another family which held possession of Riddlesden until the commencement of the seventeenth century.

How long Bingley was in the gift and feoffment of the Earls of Chester as chief lords is uncertain, but the early possession of Riddlesden by their feudatories and steady adherents, the Montalts, may be traced to the intimate connexion between the two families. And as William de Meschines, Lord of Skipton, was a sister's son of Hugh Lupus, another reason may be perceived why the township of Morton, which is in the civil jurisdiction of Skyrack was suffered by its mesne lords to become absorbed in the Skipton fee. East and West Morton, with Riddlesden, the manors comprised in the township, as may be seen in the "History of Craven," at the distant periods of 1513, 1577, and 1612, continued to be enumerated as a part of that fee. Yet, although informed by the Doctor, that "they are not to be found in the *Index Villaris* of the wapontake as it was returned into the Sheriff's office by the Earl of Burlington, and according to which all processes are directed by the Sheriff to the Bailiff of the liberty of Staincliff," he never seems to have been aware of their final separation.

According to the meagre pedigree in Thoresby's "History of Leeds" of the Paslews of Riddlesden Hall, we find that John Paslew, *vixit* third of Henry VI., son of the before-named Robert, married Amye, daughter of Mr. Beckwith. Elizabeth, daughter of John Paslew, married Thomas Hawksworth, Esq., who was living, 1444. Thomas Paslew married Jane, daughter of Sir John Neville, who was Sheriff from the third to the tenth of Henry VII.; and we find in James's "History of Bradford," that a dispute between John Lacy of Cromwell Bottom, Lord of Horton, and William Rooks of Royds Hall, respecting the boundaries of their respective manors, was referred to John Tempest of Bowling, Esq., William Paslew of Riddlesden, Esq., and two others, in the twenty-first of Henry VIII.

Stephen Paslew, probably brother of the above William, married Ann, daughter of Michael Rawden, Esq., of Rawden. Francis Paslew, *vixit*, thirty-eighth of Henry VIII, married Isabel, daughter of Sir William Calverly, Knight.

Alexander Paslew of Riddlesden, married Ellen, daughter of Thomas Lacy, Esq.; and his sister Jane married William Frank, Esq., of Alwoodley. This gentleman who appears to have resided in the neighbourhood, was buried in the chancel of Keighley church, 1578. Jane, daughter of the above-named Alexander, married Walter Hawksworth of Hawksworth, Esq., slain at Musselbro, Scotland, 10th Dec., 1547.

Walter Paslew, who appears first to have married Elizabeth, daughter of Richard Clapham, and afterwards Ellen daughter of John Lacy, Esq., left a son Francis, baptized at Keighley, 1568, who died without issue about the first of James I., leaving two sisters, Rosamond, who married John Rishworth, Esq., and —————— who married Mr. Henry Milner. John Rishworth, who succeeded his brother-in-law at Riddlesden, and who appears to have sold the estate to the Murgatroyds, was buried at Keighley, 1655.

It appears the Murgatroyds had come into possession of this place previous to the year 1640, as is shown by a stone over the door of an out-building bearing the above date, with the initials, J. M. M., S. S. M.

They are said to have been great builders, and probably ruined themselves by the stone-and-mortar mania. If we are to regard the voice of tradition, this family, by some equivocal process of law, were forcibly ejected from the place; and so strong was the popular sympathy of the neighbourhood in their favour, that the river Aire is said to have altered its course out of sullen resentment at the circumstance. According to the information furnished by another stone over the garden door, E. and H. Starkey had obtained possession and made some alterations prior to the year 1692, and from that time to the present, the Riddesden Hall property has remained in the hands of their posterity. The place is now held by two sisters and co-heirs, the elder of whom married Henry Bence Bence of Thorington Hall, county of Suffolk, Esq., and the younger a gentleman of the name of Bacon. Riddlesden Hall was long since abandoned as the family residence. Nicholas, whose spouse, Madam Starkey, was so well known on account of her singular fondness for hunting, shooting, and other masculine diversions, was the last of the family who continued to reside here. It is related of this Mr. Starkey, that once when his sporting lady had the misfortune to dislocate a joint by a fall from her horse in a hunt, in the heat of his anger, he exclaimed, with an oath, that "it was the *wrong joint*."

The Paslews of Riddlesden Hall bore, argent, a fess between three mullets, azure, pierced of the field.

The Starkeys of French Wood, county of Lancaster, and Riddlesden Hall, county of York, a younger branch of the Starkeys of Huntroyd have for their arms, argent, a bend, sable, between six storks, ppr.; crest, a stork, ppr. The Murgatroyds late of Greenhill, parish of Bingley, appear to have descended from the former owners of this place, and the Rishworths, who have long moved in a respectable sphere of life in the same parish, probably derived their surname from the district or possession of Rishworth. We find in the Keighley Parish Register, that Robert Rishworth, Gentleman, and Gilbert Drake, Yeoman, were witnesses to the marriage of John Cousin of Halifax and Miss Mary Hirst of Doncaster, in 1675.

In 1830, the Airedale Heifer, fed by Mr. Slingsby at Riddlesden Hall, was killed. This wonderful animal was slaughtered in consequence of a severe contusion on one of her hind quarters, which turned to a mortification. The owner had 400 guineas offered for her, and was to receive one-half of the profits arising from her exhibition in England. She weighed 41 stones 12lbs. per quarter, 16lbs. to the stone, and measured 11 feet 10 inches from her nose to the stump of the tail, and 10 feet 6 inches in girth. She was 11 inches deep in fat on the ribs. A sketch of this beautiful animal was taken by the late Mr. John Bradley, a native artist, and an engraving executed at a considerable expense.

WEST RIDDLESDEN HALL.

The adjacent mansion of West Riddlesden Hall, though less spacious than its venerable neighbour, is yet a fair structure in the Elizabethan style. This house was for a long time the residence of the Mauds, a younger branch from Riddlesden Hall, and, as stated by the compiler of the pedigree (who does not make the proper distinction between the two places) derives from Robert de Montalt, probably the common ancestor of Simon, the last male heir of Riddlesden Hall, and Thomas, whom we take to be the first of West Riddlesden, whose son, Constantine Monhault, or Maud, of West Riddlesden, living between the years 1480 and 1520, espoused a daughter of Thomas Kighley of Newall, and was succeeded by his son, Arthur Maud of West Riddlesden, whose will bears date 1534. "He wedded a daughter of Lawrence Townley," and had with her besides a daughter Agnes, the wife of Stephen Paslew of Rawden, a son and successor, "Thomas Monhault, or Maud, of West Riddlesden, whose will is dated 1567. This gentleman married Catharine, daughter of Roger Tempest, Esq., of Broughton, by Ann his wife, daughter of Sir John Carr, Knight, of Thornton, and grand-daughter of Thomas Lord Clifford. By this lady he had issue—Arthur Monhaut or Maud, who proved, at Glover's visitation in 1585, his descent from Constantine, and was allowed to bear his arms. He married Jane, daughter of Anthony Eltofts, Esq., of Farnhill in Craven, and had six daughters. He died 26th Dec., 1587, and was buried at Bingley."

"Christopher Maud, Esq., Holling Hall and Woodhouse, was patron of Ilkley in 1554. His will is dated 1561. He married Grace ——, and had issue Thomas of West Riddlesden, who died 3rd June, 1633. His grandson, Robert Maud, Esq., of West Riddlesden and Ripon in the county of York, patron of Ilkley, 1640, as was his father in 1607, disposed of his English estates, and purchased others in the counties of Kilkenny and Tipperary, whither he removed. He died in 1685, and was succeeded by his son, Anthony Maud, Esq., of Dundrum, M.P. for Cashell, grandfather of Sir Cornwallis Maud, Baronet, who was elevated to the Peerage of Ireland, 4th May, 1785, by the title of Baron Montalt, and created 10th June, 1791, Viscount Hawarden."

The way in which the Leaches acquired the estates of West Riddlesden borders on the romantic, and throws fiction into the shade. The last of the Mauds who reared a family was the father of seven sons and one daughter. The daughter danced at the marriage-feasts of her seven brothers in succession, every one of whom died childless; she survived them all, married a Leach, and carried the property over to that family. This was some time anterior to the year 1685. The family resided here till the year 1854, when it became extinct by the death of Mr. William Leach, the last of two worthy brothers, who had lived in harmony together three-quarters of a century.

That holy man of God, Oliver Heywood of Coley near Halifax, one of the 2000 ejected ministers of 1662, whose burning zeal could not be quenched by persecution, found a short refuge here from the pursuit of his enemies.

The West Riddlesden Hall estate was purchased a few years ago of the late Thomas Leach by the late John Greenwood, Esq., of Knoll, Keighley; it now belongs to his son, Frederick Greenwood, Esq., and is at present in the occupation of Mr. John B. Sidgwick, son-in-law of the above-named Mr. John Greenwood.

A small church was lately erected here entitled, 'St. Mary's, Riddlesden.' It is in the new district of Morton and incumbency of the Rev. William Fawcett, B. A.

THE ALTAR AND HAMLET OF MARLEY.

The Altar, situated on the heights between Keighley and Bingley and not far from the latter place, is a prominent and rocky precipice composed of huge blocks of millstone-grit rising in quick acclivity from the right bank of the river Aire, and forming one of the finest sights for grandeur and variety of interest which this picturesque vale affords. The pure bracing air on this craggy head, and the extensive and diversified scenery of wild and striking combinations of moorland summits, swelling knolls, shady woods, deep glens, and gurgling rills descending the verdant slopes to the 'bright river' as it sweeps past the busy haunts of men in a thousand curvatures, amid fertile meadows and corn-fields, amply compensate the thousands of pedestrian visitors for the toil of ascent. In addition to the name which it bears we have the evidence of a venerated tradition in support of the belief, that this place was once connected with the dark and mysterious worship of the Druids; and as a proof of the prevailing notion, it may be stated, that when between forty and fifty years ago great quantities of stone were sent from hence to the docks at Liverpool, Mr. Hartley and a number of gentlemen about Bingley, in their anxiety for its preservation, succeeded in prevailing upon the then lord of the manor to desist, though to his own manifest loss and disadvantage. The large stone pointed out as the spot where the sacrifices were wont to be offered, probably served as the pedestal of the wicker colossus in which were enclosed the doomed and trembling victims, said to have been sometimes offered under the mistaken idea of appeasing the wrath of an offended Deity. The other great stone, the surface of which is covered with the chiseled initials of numerous visitors, was most likely used as a platform for the officiating priests while performing their mysterious ceremonies and delivering their injunctions to the awe-struck multitude below. Should it be objected that the ancient Druids studied their mysteries and performed their religious rites in the 'sacred grove,' yet it will not be denied that they had their rocking-stones and rude altars on the adjacent heights; besides, the trees of the native wood, which are only separated from this place by a single fence, still wave their rugged branches over the intervening declivity down to the margin of the river.

There is another place in the vicinity which we think ought to be noticed in connexion with the Altar, called Bellbank, also a "relique of the Druids, where the Beltien-fires were kindled at certain periods of the year in honour of the sun." We are informed by a learned historian, that "on May-eve the Druids made enormous fires on the eminences, which being always to be seen from their respective situations, afforded an enlivening prospect over the whole nation. These illuminations were in honour of *Beal* or *Bealan*, the Irish and Celtic word for the sun, which the Romans latinized into *Belenus*, and applied to the same deity, as appears from several inscriptions found on monuments." Lysons, on the authority of Pennant, says, that "the Bel-tien superstition was kept up till of late years in the neighbourhood of Keswick, and that in this rural sacrifice, it was customary for the performers to bring with them boughs of mountain ash." Baal-fire was kindled on May-day evening in Ayrshire as late as 1790; and it is still faintly observed in Ireland and the Highlands of Scotland. Below this rocky eminence is to be seen the retired and almost inaccessible village of Marley, with its venerable old hall.

Marley, though not a Domesday manor, is mentioned in that great national survey as a place within the soke of Bingley, containing one carucate of land, but returned as waste. This village at an early period seems to have given name to a family; for in the ninth of Edward II., a "Peter de Marthley and Ralph de Ilketon" were lords of the adjoining manor of Morton. This place was for some time the residence of the Currers, and, as stated in the pedigree, "William Currer of Marley, who married Isabel, daughter of Christopher Maud, Esq., of Holling Hall, was the son of the first Hugh Currer of Kildwick, and elder brother of Henry of Kildwick, who died 19th Aug., 1568." And we find in the "History of Craven,"— "The manor of Bingley was sold to the Walkers, and by them to Hugh Currer of Marley, whose grandson, Henry Currer, Esq., of Gawthorpe, in the year 1668, sold it to Robert Benson, father of the first Lord Bingley." There is also a farm belonging to the Marley estate still bearing the name of 'Currer Laith;' but it appears to have entirely escaped the notice of antiquarians that Marley Hall was once the honoured abode of a Saville. This house was rebuilt by John Saville in the year 1627, whose arms and initials are still to be seen in several places. Miss Saville was married at Keighley, 1606, to Mr. Dean, son of the Bishop of Ossory in Ireland, who was then Dean of Kilkenny.* The wife of J. Saville was

---

* Richard Dean was son of Gilbert Dean of Sattonstall in the parish of Halifax, by Elizabeth, daughter of Edmund Jennings of Silsden, in the parish of Kildwick. He was made Dean of Kilkenny, in Ireland, in the year 1609, succeeded Dr. Horsfall in the Bishopric of Ossory, and died on

buried at Keighley, 1633. This family, as was common with the great and affluent of that period, maintained their hal or jester to go on errands, amuse, and entertain the visitors, and the noted 'Sil o' Marley' is still traditionally remembered by the inhabitants of the surrounding neighbourhood. It is related, that as he was carrying into the distant fields a number of pies for the dinner of the labouring men, his appetite stimulated by the delicious odour of his burden—the Bingley bells began to chime; and, 'as the fool thinketh, the bell tinketh,' to him they said most audibly, "Eat pies, Sil,—eat pies, Sil;" to which invitation he as plainly and audibly responding "Yes, and I will,—yes, and I will," sat himself down and so manfully discussed the contents, that when he arrived at his journey's end there was nothing left but the mutilated remains to place before the eyes of the hungry and disappointed ploughmen. On another occasion, Sil having been sent with a gentleman, by whom he had been much teazed during the day, to the river side, in order to show him the passage or ford, conducted him in a contrary direction, and to the deepest part of the water. The gentleman on observing this, cried out with impatience, "How, you silly rascal, how must I get over here?" to which interrogation Sil coolly and provokingly replied, "You must swim over, swim over, Sir; Mr. Saville's *geese* always swim over.

But whilst dwelling over the singularities of this once noted though degraded menial, we have yet to inquire, who was John Saville?—Was he the same person as Sir John Saville of Howley, the influential West-Riding Magistrate? or to what branch of that once powerful Yorkshire family did he belong? We suspect that he was in the commission of the peace, and that it was from his residence at Marley that Walter Calverly, the homicide, was committed. We find in the narrative of that dreadful transaction, inserted by Whitaker in the "Loides and Elmete," the following passage:—"He was thence committed to one Maister Key's house, a jaile built up in Wakefield, for at this time the infection of the plague was violent in York. The way to Wakefield from Sir John Saville's lay directly before Master Calverly's house, against which, when he came, he entreated that he might speak to his wife before he came to prison." The Doctor, in a note upon this passage, says,—"This proves that the writer was not an inhabitant of the neighbourhood, otherwise he must have known that Calverly lay in the opposite direction from Howley." Now, if we bring the parties from Howley to Marley, the passage in the narrative will not only appear substantially correct, but it will also prove the general acuteness of the Doctor's observations.

The Parkers, for many years proprietors of the capital estate of Marley, held the joint lordship denominated 'Harden-cum-Marley, Cow-house, and Cullingworth,' including, besides the cultivated land, the whole of that extensive common called 'Harden Moor. Edward Parker, Esq., of Browsholme, married Mary, daughter of Richard Sunderland, Esq., of High Sunderland, in the parish of Halifax, 28th January, 1629, sister of Samuel and Peter, the benefactors. He died, 1667. Robert, his second son, who lived at Carlton and Marley Hall, married Jane, daughter of William Rookes, Esq., of Roydes Hall, and died without posterity. The Lord of Harden-cum-Marley and Samuel Sunderland, Esq., Lord of the adjoining manor of Hainworth, caused the boundary stones to be set up, bearing their respective initials, and still serving to divide the two lordships. We are informed in Thoresby's Diary that Robert Parker, who was himself an assiduous collector of coins, succeeded to the valuable collection of Mr. Brearcliffe of Halifax. This Robert, who seems to have inherited the benevolent disposition of his uncle, left certain lands in Keighley for the endowment of an hospital at Waddington, known here by the name of 'Hospital Lands.' The Parkers had formerly considerable influence in this town, as the following and some other passages in Gale's Manuscript will show—"Jan. 19th,—there came to William Laws, at the White Horse, Mr. Parker de Carleton, Justice Parker de Browsome, Lawyer Currer, and Benjamin Ferrand, to see the foundation of our school laid, but it was not done by reason of the Parish Feoffees, who would not consent to my figure of twenty yards long, the model of which was before us.

The Parkers bear—vert, a cheveron between three stags' heads, cabossed, or.

Marley Hall estate was sold during the year 1842, by Mr. Parker of Selby to Mrs. Sarah Ferrand of St. Ives, in the parish of Bingley. The name of this village is no doubt derived from *mere*, a small lake, and *ley*, a field. The soft low ground on the west side of the hill on which the hamlet stands, together with the Bingley Bog, were probably the two last portions of an extensive lake which once spread over the whole area of Riddlesden pastures, and dammed up far above the town of Keighley. Here are two large mounds of sand and other deposits washed from the escarpments of the adjacent hill, and left by the retiring waters of the plain to puzzle the inquiring countryman how they got there and assumed such shapes. One of them is now intersected by the railway, and the sand being highly appreciated for making mortar is fast disappearing.

HAINWORTH.

HAINWORTH is another manor and village in the parish of Bingley, which, on account of its proximity to this town, we shall briefly notice. This place is the Hagenewuorde of the Domesday Survey, which Baldwin, the translator, mistakes for Haworth, and was given, by the Conqueror to Ernegis de Buron, together with Cullingworth, Bingley, and the several places within the soke of Bingley, We are informed that Hagen or Hagenworth in Saxon times meant a fenced farm or place surrounded with fences. But why called the fenced farm? was not the term equally applicable to any other farm? The following passage from the pages of a distinguished antiquarian may be deemed a sufficient answer to the inquiry:—" We learn from the decisive evidence of charters, that for three or four centuries after the Conquest there were no inclosures, excepting that the tofts or insulated messuages had each a croft annexed to them; even the meadow grounds lay in common. Next to these was the cornfield of the township, occupied in the growth of wheat, barley, oats, flax, and hemp. At a greater distance, and separated by a wall, was the common pasture for cattle; and beyond, a wide waste of moor and fell grazed by sheep. This arrangement undoubtedly took place on the general distribution of property after the Saxon conquest, and with the exception of enclosèd meadows, it subsisted in some parts of Wharfedale within the last thirty years." In Domesday, Hainworth was estimated at half a carucate, but lying waste. It was once a part of the possessions of that munificent individual, Samuel Sunderland, Esq., and was purchased of the heirs of the late Sir George Cook, Bart., by John Greenwood, Esq., of Knoll, near Keighley; and it now belongs to his son, Frederick Greenwood, Esq., of Norton Conyers.

Mr. Sunderland, who during the latter part of his life resided at a place called Hill-end, in Harden, about a mile distant from this place, was the son of Richard Sunderland, Esq., Justice of the Peace, 17th James I., by Susannah, "daughter of Sir Richard Sattonstall, Lord Mayor of London, 1597, and born in the year 1600. He went to London, where he carried on the business of a Woollen Draper, in which trade he was eminently successful, became an Alderman, and paid the fine, exempting him from serving the office of Sheriff. After he relinquished his commercial pursuits, he resided at. Harden, near Bingley, and died, 1676." The following account of his benefactions is copied from the Appendix to Thoresby's "History of Leeds."

"My ancient friend, Robert Parker, Esq., having obliged the public with his own generous benefactions, must be gratified by a present recital of those of his uncle, Samuel Sunderland, Esq., viz.—to a school of this town of Wortley, £6.; to Coley Chapel, £1.; to Idle Chapel, £8.; to Thornton Chapel, and School, £12.; to Halifax Vicarage, £10.; to Baildon Chapel, £9.; to the poor of Norwood Green, £3.; to Hipperholme School, £18.; to the Church at Bingley, £22.; to the School, £7., and to the Poor there, £6.; in all,

£107. per annum. All which the said worthy gentleman, his executor, saw faithfully performed, and delivered the writings to the respective trustees."

The annexed account of a most daring and singular robbery committed on his premises will be found in Edward Parson's "Civil and Miscellaneous History of the District within ten miles of Leeds." We trust no apology will be necessary for transferring it to our pages.

"Samuel Sunderland, Esq., who flourished in the reign of Charles I. and in the Commonwealth, resided at Harden Hall, not far from Bingley. He was one of the richest men of his age, and had accumulated an enormous quantity of gold coin which he preserved in bags placed on two shelves in a private part of his house. Two individuals, who resided at Collingham, and who were in circumstances above want, though not above temptation, determined to rob Mr. Sunderland of the whole, or at any rate of a considerable quantity, of his gold ; and in order to prevent the chance of successful pursuit, they persuaded a blacksmith at Collingham to put shoes on their horses' feet backwards way. They arrived at Harden Hall, and, according to their purpose, took away as much gold in bags as they thought they could carry off, and notwithstanding the communication of an alarm to the family before they left the house, they succeeded in accomplishing their retreat. The weight of the gold they took away was too heavy for their jaded horses, and they were compelled to leave part of it on Black Moor, where it was afterwards found by some persons of Chapeltown, whose descendants are still living at that village at the present day. It so happened that the robbers had taken a dog with them on their expedition, and this animal, in the hurry of their retreat, they left behind them fastened up in the place from which they had taken the gold. The friends and neighbours of Mr. Sunderland, who had determined upon pursuit, immediately saw in this dog the means of detecting the offenders. Having broken one of its legs to prevent it running too fast for their horses, they turned it loose. It proceeded, notwithstanding its excruciating pain, to Collingham, and went directly to the house of its owners. The pursuers arrived, burst open the door, and found the thieves in the very act of counting the money. They were sent to York, tried, and condemned to die; and their own apprentice was compelled to act the part of their executioner. This young man, though innocent of any capital participation in the robbery, was so horror-struck by the deed he had been compelled to perform, that he criminated himself and followed the fate of his masters."

"Mrs. Mary Midgley, wife of S. Midgley, Esq., of Moortown, and niece of Mr. Sunderland, immediately repaired to her uncle when she heard of the robbery, and was accustomed to relate how he had taken her to see the bags of gold which were left after the robbers had completed their work."

We observe a trifling difference between this account and the tradition of the neighbourhood where the burglary was committed. It is said Mr. Sunderland did not live at Harden Hall, but at Hill-end, in or near Harden, and that the principal part of the treasure was abstracted from a carved oak chest, now in the possession of, and sometimes shown as a curiosity by, Mr. Thomas Rishworth, lately of Thwaites, now of Tuam, Ireland. Also that the animal left behind, and which led to the discovery, was the means, as intended by the burglars, of corrupting the fidelity or lulling the vigilance of a ferocious dog, which had been held in great esteem by its owner. It appears, too, that the booty was divided at a public-house in Collingham, which gave rise to the saying, "Like the landlord of Collingham, you'll come in for your share."

Hainworth stands on a considerable eminence, though sheltered by still higher ground; and from Cradle-edge, the most elevated ridge, rising 975 feet above the sea, may be seen, as we are informed, three of the highest hills in Craven. A small edifice has been erected in this hamlet serving as a Sunday School and Methodist Chapel: and a little below, adjoining the Halifax-road, the Methodists have another moderately large building called the Wesley Place Chapel, which is also used for a Sunday and week-day school. Both these places, though in the parish of Bingley, stand within a mile and a half of the town of Keighley.

HERMIT HOLE AND GOFF WELL.

On the side of this hill a little to the south-west of Hainworth, there is a place called Hermit Hole. We know nothing of the solitary individual who chose to spend his days in some hole or cell on the slope of this valley; its seclusion and the pure rippling spring which here gushes out of the hill, and the wild but picturesque scenery of the landscape, undoubtedly induced him to erect his cross here, sanctify the site, and take up his abode.

Hermits were thought to hold intimate intercourse with heaven, work miracles, and cure diseases. Though their mode of life was professedly one of much self-denial and holy contemplation,

> "The moss their bed, the cave their humble cell,
> Their food the fruits, their drink the crystal well;
> Remote from men, with God they passed their days,
> Prayer all their business, all their pleasures praise."

Yet they often fell into vicious courses and luxurious indulgence, and instead of a blessing they became a curse. They had sometimes gardens and lands upon which they worked; and a few decayed plum-trees lately grubbed up here, and which were considered old a hundred years ago, may be not unreasonably deemed the relics of a garden kept by the holy man. Hermit Hole, properly so called, consists of a farm house and six cottages, though a large row of new houses on the line of road just beneath is now generally included in the name.

East of this place, on the skirts of Harden Moor, is a farm house known by the name of Goff Well; and as *goff* is said to be the Danish term for red, it would probably be no great stretch of the imagination to suppose the hermit was so named on account of his red hair, and the spring or well designated after him from the frequency and sanctimonious nature of his visits.

It appears that springs and fountains have from almost the earliest account of time, been looked upon as sacred, especially if their waters were medicinal; for then the priests were furnished with an argument for enforcing the paying of a religious regard thereto, as if their virtue proceeded from the local presence of some deity. Every notable well was dedicated to some particular saint, to whose merits any cures that might have been effected were always attributed; and on the saint's day whose name the well bore, the people in former times assembled there to make offerings or vows to the same, which afterwards was changed into the custom of adorning the well with boughs and flowers, and entertaining themselves with music, dancing, eating cakes, and drinking ale. We deem this to be one of the customs "better kept in the breach than the observance," though distance, like a fairy-wand, adds a charm to these rural scenes, which frequently beguiles poetic fancy into utterances whose glowing beauties rivet the attention, warm the imagination, fill the soul with pleasing emotions, and extort the exclamation—

> "Old customs, oh! I love the sound,
> However simple they may be:
> Whate'er with time hath sanction found
> Is welcome, and is dear to me."

THE RECTORS OF KEIGHLEY.

IT is to be regretted that so little is known of the former Rectors of this place; scarcely a vestige remains of any anterior to Mr. Gale, of whom we have been able to gather only a few scattered notices. Respecting our last Rector, we shall have more information to communicate, having gleaned some interesting reminiscences from his intimate friends who are yet alive to recount his good deeds.

The following brief record of Mr. Gale, whose name is still respected by many of the parishioners, with a

REV. MILES GALE.

short account of his learned son, Judge Gale, may be new to many and not unworthy of their attention, his son being the second lawyer of station and eminence mentioned in the course of this work, which may be fairly claimed either as natives, or persons intimately connected with the parish.

Miles Gale, M. A., Rector of Keighley from 1680 to 1720—1, was the son of Mr. John Gale, a descendant of the Gales of Scruton and Masham, who had been in the Low Country wars under Count Mansfield, and who in the time of James I., when Colonel Sir Thomas Danby was serving against the Scots, occupied the post of Captain, but afterwards refusing a commission from Cromwell, he retired to Farnley Hall. His elder brother's son was the learned Dr. Thomas Gale, Dean of York, father of the distinguished Roger. Miles, the Rector of Keighley, "of whose ingenious workmanship," says Thoresby, "I have a notable specimen amongst the curiosities of this Museum," was born at Farnley Hall, and married Margaret, daughter of Christopher Stone, D. D., Chancellor of York. Christopher, their eldest son, who married Sarah, relict of Harvey, Governor of North Carolina, was Attorney General and Judge of the Admiralty in that province, 1712; and in 1721 was, as we find in the diary and correspondence of the above-named author, Chief Justice of Providence and all the Bahama Islands. Mr. Gale was found dead in bed on the 2nd of January, 1720—1. On the 11th of the following February, we find the Leeds' Antiquary visited again by Judge Gale and Captain Danby,[*] to see the collections. Mr. Gale, who ap-

[*] He was one of the Denbighs of Wogan Fold or Denbigh Square, now a portion of the Market Place, and an officer in the army of Queen Anne.

pears to have been more noted for his ingenuity and general activity than for his abilities as an antiquary, was the steady friend and confident of Mr. Gyles, the eminent Glass Painter of York. His monument, formerly in this church, and luckily copied by Dr. Whitaker, was, with some others, taken away in 1805, and never found its way back; and now when there is ample room for its reception, it is strangely and unaccountably lost. Thomas, another of Mr. Gale's sons, was Rector of Linton, in Craven, and died 1750.

The appended list of the several articles contributed by Mr. Gale to Thoresby's Museum, affords at least sufficient evidence of the mental activity and mechanical skill of the contributor:—

"Memoirs of the family of Gale, particularly of the learned Dr. Thomas Gale, Dean of York, and Christopher Gale, Esq., her Majesty's Attorney General in North Carolina, 1703. A description of the parish of Keighley, writ by the Rev. Miles Gale, Rector there, whose autograph and present it is. A Reel, with silk and silver twist wound upon it after it was enclosed in a small bottle; the cork is also fastened on the inside with three wood pins. He also sent me a Hexapode, of six different pieces, fastened without glue or nails, yet not now to be severed, with the best turned tobacco-stopper, all of his own workmanship. He likewise contributed the Pyrites from Camel Cross, upon the highest hill between the east and west seas, as is evident from the springs running thence into both of them. This is called mundick by some, but it is really pyrites in the opinion of that great naturalist, Dr. Lister."

For the credit of Leeds and honour of the county, it is to be hoped that his memoirs of the family of Gale survived the wreck of Thoresby's Museum, where they had been confidently deposited, as in a secure place, for the future use of the biographer.

Mr. Gale, who held possession of the Rectory longer than any of his predecessors, was far exceeded in the duration of his incumbency by Mr. Knowlton; the former retaining the living forty and the latter sixty-one years.

MEMOIR OF
THE REV. THEODORE DURY.

THE Reverend Theodore Dury, M.A., formerly Rector of this parish, and late of West Mill, Hertfordshire, a name dear to many persons and embalmed in the hearts of some, was the third son of Alexander Dury, Esq., of Hadley, Middlesex, formerly a Lieutenant Colonel in the Coldstream Guards. His ancestors were of French extraction, and being firm adherents to the protestant faith, they suffered severely under the cruel persecutions of Louis the 14th, consequent upon the revocation of the edict of Nantes, in 1685. Although the protestant laity were forbidden under the most rigorous penalties, to quit the kingdom, the ancestors of Mr. Dury escaped to England, the asylum of thousands of their suffering brethren and the most industrious and useful subjects of the intolerant Louis; and in submission to the will of Providence they finally settled in this country.

The subject of this memoir was born at Hadley, in the year 1789. In early life he was marked by a sweet and gentle disposition, warm attachments, great buoyancy of spirit, and cheerful obedience to parental authority,—traits of character lovely in all but beautiful in youth. A fear of offending God and the awful consequences of sin would, at times, so affect his tender feelings as to make him weep profusely,— a striking feature, significantly foreshadowing the future tender-hearted parent and sympathizing pastor.

He was educated at Harrow, co-temporary with the late Lord Byron, the late Duke of Devonshire, and the Dean of Ripon. From thence he was removed to Pembroke College, Cambridge, where he graduated in due course. He was ordained to the curacy of Totteridge, near Barnet, Middlesex; and after a short time his noble friend and school-fellow, the Duke of Devonshire, presented him to the rectory of Keighley, which was rendered vacant by the death of the Rev. C. Knowlton, in the year 1814.

Mr. Dury brought to bear upon his new sphere of labours a mind well stored with human learning, but he did not possess that clear light of the gospel and that joyous evidence of its saving truths which he soon after obtained. He possessed good personal qualifications for a parish priest. His kind and affectionate disposition, his gentle temper and winning manners, combined with his ardent desire to do good according to the best of his ability, were excellent features of his character, and they carried him a certain way towards ministerial success; for these qualities seldom fail in producing something after their own image. Besides, his biblical studies had given him a general knowledge of the grand scheme of man's deliverance from sin and death by the blood and righteousness of the Lord Jesus Christ; he knew something, also, of the necessity of sanctification by the Spirit of God, and of being made a new creature in Christ Jesus; but the life and power of these views he knew not. Unfortunately, the spiritual condition in which he found the little flock of his new cure was far from cheering. Like the Laodiceans, they were neither hot nor cold, but simply indifferent, and many of them wishful to remain so. He saw this with sorrow mingled with pity; and well-knowing that the tendency of such apathy was downwards, rather than upwards, he resolved to infuse more life into them, with a view to raise them to a higher standard and enjoy the blessing of the reflex action in himself, in order to incite him to further efforts and sustain him in their progress. His aim was their improvement and prosperity, and the removal of his own imperfections. The critical ground on which he stood at this time, his transitional state of mind, his settled purpose to be useful, and his habitual yearning after ministerial ability, present him to us in the interesting light of one seeking after the right way, if haply he might find it; our sympathies are irresistibly enlisted in his favour, and we watch with eager solicitude every event in his future career, fully persuaded that he cannot be far from the full light of the kingdom of God. His earnestness in the discharge of his duties, and some trifling changes which he deemed it needful to make provoked opposition. For instance, when he, instead of the clerk, gave out the hymn after the sermon, a certain person of influence always left the church in wrathful displeasure, and often with imprecations upon the minister's head. This reprehensible conduct was a dangerous snare laid by Satan to excite the anger and imbitter the feelings of the young pastor, and urge him to retaliate in a kindred spirit, and thereby bring guilt upon his conscience, increase his difficulties, and impede his usefulness; but God mercifully preserved him from the danger: and when his heart afterwards became enriched with the gift to breathe the effectual fervent prayer of the righteous, he had the satisfaction of numbering this opponent among his steadfast friends.

His parochial visitations also frequently presented the bitter before the sweet. Under such trials he felt the need of heavenly wisdom for counsel, light for guidance, strength for support, and grace for comfort. The discipline was too severe for mere morality and good intentions; dejection of mind and self-reproaches naturally ensued, unrelieved by that heart-felt satisfaction which the Holy Spirit imparts to the truly devout, under similar conflicts. His courteous demeanour and conciliatory spirit enabled him to surmount many external difficulties incident to his position; but the silent monitions of conscience warned him of a greater difficulty in his own heart than any he could find in his outward circumstances. To remove that difficulty eventually became the all-absorbing theme.

In the course of his pastoral visits he occasionally conversed with a few plain, intelligent christians of the Wesleyan persuasion, who, as he once remarked at a missionary meeting, when reciting the Lord's dealings with his soul, were the chief means under God of opening his eyes to see his real condition, as a sinner, and excite the cry "What must I do to be saved?" With an aching heart and tearful eye, he diligently besought the Lord to "cleanse the thoughts of his heart by the inspiration of his Holy Spirit," and grant unto him the joys of a present salvation. At this time, the counsels of a dying saint proved a special help and blessing to his penitent soul. He directed him in joyful accents to the "Lamb of God which taketh away the sins of the world," and entreated him to take no rest until he had found the pearl of great price, and felt the power of that faith and love which had borne himself through the heat and burden of the day, and which now sustained his departing soul and opened unto him an ineffable prospect of everlasting happiness and glory. The word was spoken in due season, and it was not long ere Mr. Dury found that peace of mind which passeth all understanding. He could now rejoice with joy unspeakable and full of glory, and appropriate by faith the inestimable benefits and privileges of the christian's charter, "For all things are yours; whether Paul, or Apollos, or Cephas, or the world, or life, or death, or things present, or things to come; all are yours, and ye are Christ's, and Christ is God's." The sacred oracles now beamed with a glorious light which opened to him the import of many passages that had hitherto been difficult and obscure, and gave such a lustre to the gracious message of salvation as produced in him the liveliest emotions of love and admiration. He found that Wisdom hath mingled her wine and furnished her banquet with more delectable things for the life of the soul, the enjoyment of the heart, and the pleasures of the understanding, than he had any previous conception of. Having found Christ to be the way by his example, the truth by his word, and the life by his grace, he delighted to sit at his feet, like Mary of old, to hear the words of eternal life, and to meditate upon his holy and blessed character, his offices, power, and faithfulness, and the harmony and glory of the divine perfections manifested through him to the church. The more he looked at him, the more he loved him, and the more he loved him, the more he desired to know of him. Daily and copiously did he drink at the fountain of living waters, the streams whereof make glad the city of God.

These renovated feelings and fresh sources of light

gave him new views of the aspects of nature and the events of Providence, which, to a mind so susceptible of impressions from the beauties of creation, and the wisdom and goodness of God displayed therein, must have added considerably to the measure of his happiness.

Having tasted of the goodness of the Lord and felt the powers of the world to come, replenished with the unction of the Holy Ghost, and rejoicing in the love of God shed abroad in his heart, he sought to bring all his flock into the same happy state. United to God by a living faith through Jesus Christ, and animated and supported by the agency of the Holy Spirit, he wearied not in well-doing nor counted his life dear so that he might serve God his Saviour by bringing many souls to glory. He "warned every man and taught every man in all wisdom," testifying in season and out of season repentance towards God and faith in our Lord Jesus Christ—inculcating the necessity of an entire surrender of the heart to God with all its hopes and fears, and describing in plain but glowing language the privileges of believers, the beauties of holiness, the pleasures of piety, and the nature of true happiness. All the great doctrines of the Bible were duly brought before his hearers, and urged as motives to obedience and adoration; their scope and spirit developed, enforced, and vindicated; their mutual dependence and harmony exhibited, and the agreement of our beautiful liturgy with their teaching demonstrated. But his favourite theme, as it is that of all eminent christians, was the glorious work of Redemption. On this attractive and mysterious subject all his affections centred; and no marvel, for who that has experienced its blessed effects does not refresh his soul and see more cause for wonder, love, and praise, every time he contemplates that which angels desire to look into? The seed sown in faith and prayer soon sprang up and bore a glorious harvest of precious fruit. Many of all ages were brought to a knowledge of the truth as it is in Jesus, some of whom are now rejoicing with their Spiritual Father in the realms above, and some are on their way to join them.

To none, however, is the cup of life one of unmixed sweetness, and the path all flowery in this inconstant state. Dark clouds often gather and suddenly overcast the brightest sky; but let the tempest rage and the billows swell, the Christian, with the sheet-anchor of hope, outrides the storm, and again enjoys the gentle gale which wafts him to the haven of rest. Religion does not exempt the Christian from calamity and suffering, but it fortifies the mind against them, and infuses a softening balm into the wounds of the spirit; it does not repress feelings in affliction, but sanctifies them under the ordeal.

In the year 1820, Mr. Dury was called to mourn over the sickness and death of his amiable and accomplished wife, who during five years had shared in his joys and sorrows. She had born him three children, but only two survived her, a son and a daughter. He felt the pang of separation to be a sore trial, but he did not mourn as those without hope; she left a good testimony of her acceptance in the Beloved, and that comforted him. Her demise took place at Hastings, where she had gone for the benefit of the air; and his desire to smooth her dying pillow and administer the last consolations of religion induced him to employ a curate in his absence. The Providence of God led him to a fit substitute in the person of the Rev. John Bickers, a man like himself, ever watching for opportunities to do good.

At this period there was no evening service at the church, and as Mr. Bickers was walking out one sabbath evening, he noticed a number of young men and boys playing on the road. The thought struck him that he might be useful to them. He entered into conversation with them on the nature of the sabbath and the duty of keeping it holy. His remarks being offered in a cheerful and familiar way were well received, and he invited them to come to the Rectory next sabbath evening, to read a portion of God's word. At the appointed hour on the following sabbath several of them came, and they spent an agreeable season together; and every returning sabbath he had the happiness to see an increase. On Mr. Dury's return, he cordially approved of the work, and engaged in it with all his heart. The room at the Rectory soon became too small for the growing numbers. A house at Damside was then fitted up by the late Mr. Sugden, of Eastwood House. Here they formed a regular Sunday school, with a proper staff of teachers, but, like the sons of the prophets in the school of Elisha, they found the place too strait for them, whence they removed to a large room at Mill Hill; and this in its turn gave place to the present large and eligible National School buildings.

Never did a finer field present itself to Mr. Dury for the display of his talents than this nursery of the church of Christ. Every qualification requisite for a shepherd over the lambs of his flock seemed to meet in him. A goodly person, a smiling countenance, a warm heart, a love for children, unaffected simplicity and condescension, a winning manner, unrelaxing perseverance, and a burning zeal for the salvation of souls. His instructions and addresses were clear, appropriate, and fervent, replete with illustrations from the daily events of life and the wide domain of natural objects, rich in anecdotal matter, and delivered with that melting pathos which invariably moves the heart and secures the love of youth; they were eminently adapted to inform the mind, convict the conscience, and lead the scholar into the ways of pleasantness and paths of peace. His skilful method of vivifying sacred subjects, especially of picturing out scriptural characters and presenting them prominently to the mind in the most lovely and fascinating aspects, insensibly drew out of the hearts of the more thoughtful children longing desires to be like them, and serious resolves to give themselves to God. The school was assembled three times on the sabbath day, and the evening season was frequently thronged by persons desirous to witness the lovely sight and hear the catechetical instruction and lectures then given. His familiar acquaintance with geography, history, and natural science, enabled him to invest those portions of scripture relating to such subjects with an interest captivating to the fancy and profitable to the hearts of parents as well as of children. A friend, who was a scholar in his school, and who left Keighley at the early age of twelve years, thus writes to us:—" Hundreds besides myself could never think any Sunday school like his. He was always happy among children, and ready to blend entertainment with instruction. I well remember his gentle hand being laid on my head with the compliment, 'Good boy,' on the occasion of repeating a collect or answering some question in the reading lesson. Though the school was very large, there were seldom any complaints of bad behaviour at church. I was a scholar in Master Theodore's class, and the good lessons which that pious youth gave me I hope to remember to my dying day. It is more than probable that, had I not been under his teaching, I should not have occupied my present position of trust and importance."

Whatever suggestions could be made for perfecting the agency of the Sunday school system were freely adopted; and sensible of the greater efficiency of teachers whose minds are furnished with suitable knowledge for their responsible duties, and that knowledge sanctified by the graces of the heart, he met his teachers on a week-day evening for the purpose of preparing the Sunday lessons, social intercourse, mutual encouragement, and prayer. He rightly considered the school as a part of the congregation, and he ever aimed to drop a word of counsel and comfort into the heart of the child whilst administering the word of life to the people at large. He esteemed it a high privilege to publish the glad tidings of salvation from the pulpit and offer the message of peace and love to riper age, but he seemed to be in a freer air and happier mood when feeding the lambs of Christ in the school-room. Listen to his words:—
"If angels are capable of envy they would feel this passion when they see the teachers in a Sunday-school busily and devoutly employed in leading their scholars to Christ, that they may be saved for ever; but angels are only permitted to *wait* until the penetential tear is called forth by the awakening voice of the affectionate teacher. If there is joy in the pre-

sence of the angels of God over one sinner that repenteth, much more ought there to be joy among those who have been the instruments under God of bringing, not one, but many sinners to repentance. Such is the joy of the teachers and officers of this school. Four children have been taken from it during the past year and translated into the paradise above."

What a numerous company of glorified spirits walking the golden streets of the New Jerusalem in the regions of everlasting blessedness were born here. The recording angel beautified the pages of the book of life with yearly accessions to the cloud of witnesses in heaven above, whilst their faithful pastor published their departure from the vale of tears below. The annual reports of the school and the pages of the *Monthly Teacher* amply testify to a part of those who were taken from the evil to come and made meet for the inheritance of the saints in light. Striking instances of the enlightening and sanctifying power of the Comforter, and of the influence of faith and hope in confirming and sustaining the renewed spirit in the drooping and dying body were, from time to time, manifested by those sweet flowers of heaven, as well as of the immediate good accruing to their friends and relatives. A noted clergyman being on a visit at the Rectory, in a friendly discussion on doctrinal subjects with Mr. Dury, denied the possibility of knowing our sins to be forgiven and of having the assurance of faith. On the following day he accompanied his host to the bedside of a dying scholar whom he freely questioned on the disputed subjects. The replies of the youth were so clear and forcible, his testimony so bright and convincing, that the gentleman saw his error and sought for similar evidence.

"Out of the mouth of babes and sucklings thou hast perfected praise." Secular benefits not unusually attend spiritual blessings, for "godliness has the promise of the life that now is and that which is to come." Besides the social advantages derived from the school by the scholars and teachers in general, several of the more pious and gifted of this heavenly nursery entered the sacred ministry; and its indirect effects on many of the parishioners who seldom attended any place of worship were often seen and acknowledged. At the close of Mr. Dury's incumbency, the school consisted of 550 scholars and 150 teachers. A week-day school for girls and an infant school were kept in the same place under his protection.

In the year 1835, he undertook the management and support of a Sunday school which had existed for some short time previous at Paper Mill Bridge, where he occasionally held Divine service. This resulted, under the care of his successor, in the erection of a new church and school-rooms. With the pecuniary aid of his father-in-law, the late John Greenwood, Esq., he afterwards established Sunday and week-day schools at Newsholme, and a Sunday school at Harehills, and appointed a clergyman to the united places.

In every church there is great variety of individual character as well as much disparity of Christian attainments in the members. Some are quiet and retiring, and find the services of the Sabbath and daily closet devotions, with the reading of the Scriptures, sufficient under God's blessing to nourish and increase the graces of the spirit; some are weak and doubtful, and want additional help and instruction, and more means of grace; while some are ever hungering and thirsting after righteousness, and embrace every opportunity to whet the desire and be filled. For the benefit of these two last classes, he began a course of cottage lectures in the year 1821. In these lectures he used great plainness of speech and homeliness of illustration ; he meted out a portion of heavenly food suited to the respective wants of each one of the select company, and held up faith as the root of all graces, and the want of it as the cause of our weakness and distress of heart. To nourish and strengthen this vital principle, and show its power to establish and sustain the soul, he went through the lives of those Old and New Testament saints whose history is so pregnant with lessons on this important doctrine. He taught the need of secret prayer and a careful perusal of Holy Scripture ; and how a strong and an abiding sense of the power and grace of God upon the heart would remove doubts and complaints, make hard things easy and bitter things sweet, dispose the heart cheerfully to do and suffer the whole will of God, to live upon him and to him, as our wisdom, righteousness, sanctification, and supreme end. They were admirably adapted to build up his hearers in the most holy faith.

At the close of one of these lectures he left the little group to themselves. The season had been a "time of refreshing from the presence of the Lord," and longing for a greater baptism of divine love, they united in social prayer and praise : hence the origin of prayer-meetings in connexion with the church at Keighley. Mr. Dury at once sanctioned these meetings, and warmly co-operated with his members in carrying them on ; and for their better guidance he drew up a set of rules and directions. A branch of the same stock, but under different treatment, was soon after planted and diligently cultured. This was an ordinance known by the name of conversation-meetings, which, in the course of time, and against the wishes of many members, merged into class-meetings. At those meetings, after singing and prayer, one read a portion of God's word, and conversational remarks were made upon it; then one or more related their experience, after which they closed with singing and prayer. No one was asked to give his experience; hence one strong objection against class-meetings was obviated. Much diversity of opinion exists as to whether class-meetings do really promote religion or not. It must be admitted that there is a danger of engendering hypocrisy; for, as good impressions not carried into practice tend to harden the heart, so a weekly confession of sin before a fellow-creature not seriously repented of, and consequently without true amendment of life, may gradually blunt the better feelings, extinguish the purer aspirations, and work an indefinable fear of the consequences of evil and an indistinct hope of escaping them into a sort of notional religion, and produce a mere talking formalist. The truly pious are not exposed to this charge, still a net of a finer texture is spread for their feet. Of course these objections and others which might be adduced apply in a minor degree against all the means of grace, and involve the question in more difficulties than at first sight appear. For their efficiency much depends on the character of the leaders. If the leaders are not discreet and enlightened persons, well acquainted with the human heart, plain and faithful in questioning, examining, advising, and exhorting their members, many defects and short-comings, and much spiritual blindness may be found to consist with constant attendance at class-meetings. We have a case in point which happened near this place.

A certain churchman familiarly conversing with a Wesleyan friend, a class-leader, on the subject of prayer, lamented the difficulty he sometimes felt to keep his thoughts from wandering when in his closet devotions, the latter said that no worldly thoughts ever entered his mind on such occasions. The churchman, somewhat incredulous, and wishful to awaken his friend from his delusion and show him the real state of the case, offered to give him his best cow if no forbidden thought intruded itself into his next evening prayer. With joyful anticipations of a heavenly blessing and a temporal reward, at the close of the day he prepared for worship as usual; but the first thought upon kneeling down and the last thought on rising up was the *cow*, and it was present throughout his devotions! This convinced the Wesleyan of his blindness, humbled his views, led him to self-examination, and kept him from future presumption.

The human heart is deceitful above all things, and even in the regenerate, it requires to be kept with all diligence and watchfulness unto prayer, or its natural inclination to evil will manifest itself in a thousand silent ways; and the suggestions of Satan will lead us to dwell on past experience and lull us into fancied security, until we find, when too late, like Ignorance in Bunyan's Allegory, that from the gate of heaven we are on the way to hell. Mr. Dury was alive to the abuse as well as to the good use of his own meetings, and he strove to avoid the one and reap the advantages of the other.

It might be thought that all these auxiliary means of grace to the most important service of the church—teaching in the school, lectures, prayer-meetings, and conversation-meetings—would keep his people always on the wing, and cause them to neglect their daily avocations and family and closet duties. We are not aware that it was so; though it is quite common with some persons to run from meeting to meeting, and like Pharaoh's kine, devour a great deal; but for want of proper digestion, they do not flourish; their souls are lean, and their profession abounds more in leaves than in fruit. Everything is beautiful in its season, but if one duty is allowed to jostle another out of its place, it is a sign either of a weak judgment or of a wrong turn of mind. No public ordinances can make amends for the neglect of secret prayer, meditation, study of God's word, and of due attention to our daily calling. As a faithful minister of Christ, with a deep and sometimes overwhelming sense of his heavy responsibilities, he watched over all with prayerful interest; and allowing for the defects which cling to everything earthly he had the unspeakable satisfaction to see all work together for good. The attendance at church improved, the Sunday school increased, and the work of the Lord prospered more abundantly among them.

In 1825 he founded a Samaritan society for visiting and relieving the sick poor at their own homes. Twelve females volunteered their services, two for a week in rotation, to visit the sick and needy without distinction of sect or party, to bestow pecuniary relief, impart a word of sympathy and comfort, lend suitable tracts, and mitigate distress both of body and mind. This society removed a considerable weight from his benevolent heart, as the sick and suffering parishioners were objects of his affectionate solicitude, and his strength and time quite inadequate to visit them as he wished. He did not however slacken his diligence in running on this errand of mercy; for the enlarged sphere of activity demanded proportionate labour, and the two-fold motive of duty and love ever allured him to the sick-bed and the dying-couch, where he had so often wept for joy to see the triumphs of the cross. At one time he employed a male lay-agent expressly for this work. He paid much attention to the inmates of the poor-house, whose misfortunes he commiserated and sought to alleviate by temporal comforts and spiritual counsel. He delivered a sermon or lecture at the house once a fortnight, alternating weekly with the dissenters.

As a parish priest, he was anxious for the welfare of the entire population, and he left no means untried to accomplish this end. His studious endeavour to sow beside all waters, to stimulate his regular hearers to "covet earnestly the best gifts," habituate them to a heavenly frame of mind, and cast a word to those who did not attend his ministry, induced him to print and circulate the following

HINTS FOR DAILY PRACTICE.

ENDEAVOUR continually through the course of each day, to realize the presence of God.

At the commencement of every day, calculate upon meeting with many circumstances that may disquiet and disappoint you; and see to it that you trust in the Lord, that you may not be afraid of evil tidings; for you know not what a day may bring forth.

We should live upon Christ as the life-giving root of all sanctification. Pray to the Lord, as David did, to set a watch over your lips to keep the door of your mouth, "for he that bridles not his tongue, proves that his religion is vain."

Before you speak, ask yourself these three questions:—Is what I am going to say true? Is it useful? Is it kind? When the Lord thy God is pacified towards thee, thou shalt open thy mouth no more, to boast, to censure, or to complain.

Come to the blood of Christ to have sin pardoned, then come to the arm of Christ to have it subdued; pray for a calm, composed, and considerate state of mind.

See that your temper is Christian-like, that is, kind, merciful, considerate, and cheerful, meek and affectionate; and remember if religion has done nothing for your temper, it has done little for your soul.

RULES TO BE OBSERVED BY THOSE WHO ARE DESIROUS OF BEING ESTABLISHED IN HOLINESS.

BELIEVE, without wavering, the love of God towards you in Jesus Christ. We have known and believed the love that God hath to us, for God is love.

Live by faith in your Redeemer every moment. Frequently exercise yourselves in particular acts of faith.

Preserve in your minds a rooted aversion to every kind of sin.

Guard against lightness and trifling; cultivate a seriousness of deportment.

Endeavour to retain a grateful sense of the mercies of God.

Be careful not to grieve the Holy Spirit, by which ye are sealed to the day of redemption.

Be much in the study of the Scriptures.

Be cautious of paying attention to dreams, impulses, and extraordinary frames.

Endeavour to be watchful and recollected.

Prepare for raillery and opposition. Take up the cross.

Preserve simplicity in all your actions.

Set a good example to all around you.

Let your affections and desires be regulated by the Spirit and Word of God.

Study to improve all the dispensations of God.

Prize union and fellowship with God and his Church.

Let prayer and praise fill your hearts and proceed from your lips.

Be ready, at all times, for your departure out of the body, and to be present with Jesus Christ.

How beautiful are the feet, how welcome the visits of that minister whose life is a living epistle of these choice precepts; they embody the root and matter of the gospel. From our own recollection, and the testimony of others, we believe Mr. Dury's daily walk and conversation entirely accorded with the spirit of these directions; he practised himself what he inculcated upon his people. A diary which he kept for a short time reveals the inmost workings of a heart overflowing with love to God and man; exciting tears of joy from its fulness, and lifting his affections to the upmost link of the golden chain that binds the soul to God. This love which streamed into his enraptured soul from the throne of glory, and shed its rich fragrance o'er all his path, is no abstract ideality dwelling in the imagination, and wrapping up the soul in its mythic conceptions; it is a strong, vital, gracious principle, uniting piety to humanity, diffusive and fervid as the rays of the noonday sun, melting the obdurate, subduing the stubborn, transforming the savage to a saint; a fountain of comfort to the believer, a "sovereign balm to every wound, a cordial to his fears." From this genial soil of a loving heart emanated that kindred virtue, candour, which ever constrained Mr. Dury to look with indulgence at the frailties of other people, conscious that he himself was but a frail creature, to love every one who loved the Lord Jesus Christ in sincerity, and, without compromise of principle, to co-operate with all Christian parties for the promotion of the public good. He delighted to soften down harsh things spoken of absent persons by mentioning their good qualities, or suggesting their probable existence; and when his own name was calumniated he carried the matter to the throne of grace, where love supplants all bitterness and pardons all offences.

Of the various exemplary qualities conspicuous in the character of this good man there was one shining above all the rest, aptly fitting him to be a messenger of mercy to every class in the parish, more especially to the poor, and which might justly be termed his crowning grace. It was said of John the Baptist that he was a burning and a shining light, chiefly, we apprehend, because his great humility contrasted so admirably with his more dazzling excellences. The dew-drop lies low on the ground, but its pearly disc reflects the complete image of the sun; so humility, with all its clustering graces retiring from the sight of man, reflects the brightness of the Father's countenance. Humility is the golden fruit of Christian perfection; "it is," said his friend, the philanthropic Wilberforce, "the peculiarity of the Christian religion that humility and holiness increase in equal proportion." "Less than the least of all saints" was his pervading sentiment, impressed on every action, traced in every step, exalting him to a dignity higher than that of a king, because it identified him with those whom Jesus Christ hath made to be both kings and priests unto God the Father, and inheritors of the ineffable glories of Him who is King of kings and Lord of lords. Our blessed Saviour ennobled this virtue by washing the feet of his disciples, practically showing how He who sought not his own glory would have the servant humble as his Lord. The praise of man tends to deepen genuine humility rather than to excite vanity. Frequently would the love-toned words drop from his gentle lips when a friend spoke well of his sermons or his deeds, "The weaker the instrument the more glory to God." "Blessed are the poor in spirit for theirs is the kingdom of heaven," is the first of the beatitudes, the inlet of all the good flowing to the soul of man on earth, and the divine pledge that when the mortal life of such humble saints shall end, the welcome voice of Him who has redeemed them and washed their robes white in his precious blood, will proceed from the throne of glory, saying, "Come, ye blessed of my Father, inherit the kingdom prepared for you from the foundation of the world."

Next to the joys of religion he ranked the pleasures of knowledge; and in order to excite and cultivate a taste for useful and instructive reading, and lead his young parishioners to observe, examine, and reflect on the works and word of God, he commenced a periodical publication, entitled, the "Monthly Teacher," in the year 1829, and continued it with much acceptance to the public as long as his health permitted. It was an entertaining miscellany of original articles on subjects relating to art, science and nature, Providence and religion, enriched with choice selections from approved authors. This magazine may be said to have reflected and stereotyped his own mind and heart; and it is much to be regretted that the accumulated labours which now pressed upon him so seriously affected his health as to render it expedient for him to resign its editorial care on the completion of the third volume. His friend and neighbour, the Rev. William Tiler, kindly relieved him of the charge, and engaged to carry it on in the same laudable spirit with which it had been hitherto conducted. Possessing a deep love for the physical sciences, and a due appreciation of their importance to every class of the community as instruments of education—keys to open the arcana of nature, and unveil some of the more striking laws which govern the operations of the material universe, he frequently lectured in the school-room and Mechanics' Institution on pneumatics, hydrostatics, electricity, and other branches, showing, by the aid of suitable apparatus, the application of their principles to the useful and ornamental arts, and the productions of the comforts and luxuries of civilized life.

Geography, in all its ramifications, was a favourite topic, around which he could bring from the treasures of his mind a great amount of varied and pictorial information, peculiarly adapted to call into exercise the nobler faculties of the mind, cultivate the organs of sense, augment the sources of pleasure, and subserve the interests of religion.

In the year 1838 he made some interesting experiments on electricity at a worsted mill in the town. He ascertained that when a leathern strap passed over two drums and crossed midway, so as to resemble the figure ∞, singular electrical effects were exhibited at the point of crossing. On presenting the knuckles, numerous brilliant brushes of electric light streamed off; a prime conductor drew sparks two inches in length; a large Leyden jar could be charged in a few seconds, and at any time, for the electricity was constant. He sent a communication of the discovery to his learned friend, Professor Faraday, who at once acknowledged its merits and gave it publicity. In the full persuasion that science and literature are the handmaids of religion, he was early enrolled a member of the Society for the Diffusion of Useful Knowledge, which brought him into contact with many persons distinguished in the republic of letters, with some of whom he formed valuable intimacies.

He was an occasional visitor and speaker at the London May Meetings; and although not to be classed among the eloquent orators whose brilliant speeches and thrilling appeals arouse the immense masses assembled on those occasions to noble acts of love and mercy, yet his clear and fervid language secured thoughtful attention, touched the more delicate cords of the softer feelings, and helped to give unity to the whole. These meetings were of essential personal service to him; for as "Iron sharpeneth iron; so a man sharpeneth the countenance of his friend;" and to meet in one place with such a number of zealous men, who, like himself, were settled in distant parts of the Lord's vineyard, for interchange of love, counsel, and encouragement, served to fire his soul and gird him with fresh energy for the discharge of his parochial duties. He numbered among his friends some of the most eminent evangelical ministers who took a part in these proceedings, and occasionally procured their services for his own pulpit.

Several of those societies connected with the May meetings had branch societies in Keighley—as the Bible, Religious Tract, and Missionary Societies—over which he cheerfully presided, and diligently advocated their noble designs and objects. Another society in the town received a large share of his fostering care, at the sacrifice of much peace of mind and some few friendships; but duty was his watchword, and where that led the way he hesitated not to follow. Well would it have been for the Temperance movement, if the mantle of its true friend had fallen upon some local member of equal influence and efficiency.

Though his prayers and alms ascended up as a memorial before God, and returned to him laden with the unction of the Holy Ghost, and his labours were crowned with that degree of success which would have more than sufficed for most ministers, yet his sanguine heart and zeal for the Lord of Hosts craved for more visible tokens of God's approbation and a larger increase of seals to his ministry. He worked, prayed, and wept for the salvation of his people. So extreme were his anxieties and fears lest he should be held accountable at the last day, not only for the souls of his congregation, but for those in the parish of whom he knew little or nothing, that his heart often fainted at the dreadful thought, and excited a wish for less responsibilities. He wanted to have a familiar acquaintance with every one of his parishioners, and reciprocate acts of kindness and friendship with all parties; but these desirable objects were quite unattainable in their full extent. Again and again did he kneel in prayerful counsel with Him who searches all hearts and knows all thoughts, and beseech his light and help to direct him in the way most conducive to his honour and glory. "Commit thy way unto the Lord; trust also in him, and he shall bring it to pass," is a precious passage, setting forth a relation between precept and promise which has never yet been known to fail in procuring everything suitable for the welfare of the faithful, and which was signally displayed in the present instance.

In the providence of God the living of the rural district of West Mill, Hertfordshire, in the patronage of the Earl of Mexborough, became vacant at this time; but as the vacancy was occasioned by the promotion of the incumbent to the bishopric of the Isle of Man, the next appointment fell to the crown. The present Earl of Carlisle, and the Hon. George Byng, M. P., without knowing of each other's intentions, respectively interceded with the Premier, Lord Melbourne, in behalf of Mr. Dury. His Lordship was pleased at the circumstance, and having perfect confidence in their representations, he graciously acceded to their joint appeal. This was just the sort of incumbency he had prayed for; the people were few in number, and he would be able to know them individually and bring them all within his immediate influence.

Few can tell the feelings which struggle in the heart of a devoted, faithful pastor, upon bidding adieu to the flock whose hopes and fears, joys and sorrows, have been identified with his own for twenty-six years, and among which are some bright jewels destined to shine in his crown of glory throughout the countless ages of eternity—precious gems that his heavenly Father has vouchsafed him grace and strength to polish after the similitude of a palace; social and private associations attaching the affections to every local event and incident, to every place consecrated by memories sunny or sad, and now recurring to the mind with overwhelming force, investing the scenes with a subduing interest, and creating a doubt whether flesh and blood can sever the link that binds the whole together. Over one spot he lingered with peculiar regard—the churchyard, to which he had committed so many bodies in sure and certain hope of the resurrection to eternal life, and where rested the mortal remains of his infant son, Frederick, and of his pious and beloved son Theodore. This young disciple was gifted with all the amiable traits of his surviving father and the meek graces of his glorified mother. In 1833, at the age of seventeen, it pleased the Lord to call him to join his happy mother in singing the song of Moses and the Lamb in the mansions of the blest. In life he was lovely; in death, triumphant. In his last moments, to his father's whisper, "Is Christ precious?" He replied, "More so than ever." What a cordial to the parent's heart! What a glorious testimony to the value of religion !

Mr. Dury was, however, gradually reconciled to the change by the assurance that, though separate from his dear friends and fellow-pilgrims in the body, he could be daily with them at the throne of grace, where they could bear each other upon their hearts in prayer, and anticipate the happy time when they should all meet around the throne of glory to separate no more for ever.

His candour, usefulness, habitual courtesy, and consistency of conduct, won the esteem of every Christian denomination and every influential person in the town and neighbourhood, some of whom deemed it a favour to be permitted to contribute towards the purchase of a valuable piece of silver plate, which his congregation presented to him as a memorial of that love which neither time nor distance could ever extinguish in their glowing hearts. And his unremitting services in behalf of general education were so highly appreciated by the members of the Mechanics' Institution, whose prosperity was largely indebted to his guiding hand, that they not only presented him with an appropriate token of respect, but had an excellent portrait taken of him to adorn the walls of their Institution, perpetuate their gratitude, and refresh their recollection of the great benefits which he had rendered them.

Mr. Dury left Keighley for West Mill, on the 2nd of July, 1840. He found the change from a large population to a small one to be strange to his habits and feelings, but very beneficial to his health. Though the people were comparatively few, there was much work to be done, and which he hoped by the blessing of God to do more efficiently for that very reason. His first object was to erect schools for the young. This favourite work was materially facilitated by the suavity of his manners and ardent zeal for the glory of God operating so favourably upon a gentleman of a different creed, as to elicit a spontaneous offer of £100. and ground for the site. The most happy effects resulted from his school labours in this new part of his Master's vineyard; and his ministerial work proved a marvellous light unto many immortal souls. He experienced what, we suppose, is common to agricultural places, that the people were slow to apprehend, but when once convinced they were proportionably retentive of the impression.

> "He tried each act, reproved each dull delay,
> Allured to brighter worlds and led the way."

During the ten years that he continued to serve God here, he evidenced a gradual growth in personal holiness and an advance to maturity in those Christian graces which so eminently distinguished him as a parent, minister, and friend. His lot was in a pleasant place, and his "peace did flow as a river, and his righteousness as the waves of the sea." His path was indeed "as the shining light, that shineth more and more unto the perfect day."

His love of peace and unity induced him, a little before his death, to publish a pamphlet on the agitated question of Baptism. This pamphlet breathes that very spirit of conciliation and charity which alone is wanted to settle the point in the only way it ever can be settled; and that is, by mutual forbearance and respect for one of the great trophies of the Reformation, the right of private judgment.

On Tuesday Sep. 24th, 1850, he held a service in Buntingford Workhouse, three miles from home; and feeling unwell on his return, he retired early to bed. On the two following days he grew worse, and on Friday symptoms of typhus fever appeared, and that fatal malady, brain fever, finally supervened. He lost nearly all consciousness after Friday; the few intervals of self-possession that did occur were filled up by prayer and praise, often uttering, glory, hallelujah, victory, victory! At twelve o'clock at noon on Wednesday, October 2nd, he calmly fell asleep in Jesus.

Thus passed away one of the excellent of the earth, one whose life was a beautiful model of all he taught and preached, affording a conspicuous example of the happy union and elevating power of those Christian graces which are within the reach of all. The same God who gave him richly all things to enjoy is our God; the same wells of salvation and banquet of heavenly manna which refreshed and fed him on the way, are free for us; and the same warfare in kind, in which he burnished his spiritual armour in going from victory unto victory, is ours; let us, therefore, like him, be faithful unto death, that we may likewise receive a crown of life.

In 1822, Mr. Dury contracted a second marriage with Miss Anne Greenwood, daughter of the late John Greenwood, Esq., of Keighley. By this lady, who is still living, he left five sons and two daughters; he had also one surviving daughter by his first wife. Though united to his family by the strongest bonds of mutual affection, he was willing to leave them for a season. Like Abraham, he had brought up his children and his household in the nurture and admonition of the Lord, into whose hands he prayerfully committed them, in the full assurance, through God's blessing upon his parental counsels, of meeting them all in heaven, where in the presence of rejoicing angels before the throne and the Lamb, he could say, "here are we and the children whom the Lord has given us."

Among the many demonstrations of respect paid to his memory immediately after death, one of the most pleasing and permanent was the erection of a beautiful cenotaph in the chancel of the Parish Church, Keighley, with a tablet bearing the following inscription:—

Sacred to the Memory

OF

THE REV. THEODORE DURY,

WHO ENTERED INTO HIS REST ON THE SECOND DAY OF OCTOBER, 1850,

FOR TWENTY-SIX YEARS HE WAS RECTOR OF THIS PARISH,

AND FOR TEN YEARS,

OF THE PARISH OF WEST MILL, IN HERTFORDSHIRE;

WHERE HIS REMAINS ARE INTERRED.

AS A FAITHFUL STEWARD OF THE TRUST

COMMITTED TO HIM,

HE ZEALOUSLY PROCLAIMED AMONG HIS PEOPLE THE SAVING

DOCTRINES OF THE CROSS,

IN ALL HUMILITY AND SIMPLICITY OF HEART.

ABOVE ALL, HE WAS TENDERLY SOLICITOUS IN FEEDING THE LAMBS OF CHRIST'S FLOCK, AND IN HIS LIFE AND CONVERSATION ADORNED THE SACRED DOCTRINES WHICH HE PREACHED;

"DETERMINED TO KNOW NOTHING BUT CHRIST AND HIM CRUCIFIED."

THIS MONUMENT

WAS RAISED BY

THE RECTOR, AND THE SUPERINTENDENTS,

TEACHERS, AND FRIENDS OF THE CHURCH SUNDAY SCHOOL,

TO TESTIFY THEIR GRATEFUL REMEMBRANCE OF HIM.

BIBLIOLIFE

Old Books Deserve a New Life
www.bibliolife.com

Did you know that you can get most of our titles in our trademark **EasyScript**[TM] print format? **EasyScript**[TM] provides readers with a larger than average typeface, for a reading experience that's easier on the eyes.

Did you know that we have an ever-growing collection of books in many languages?

Order online:
www.bibliolife.com/store

Or to exclusively browse our **EasyScript**[TM] collection:
www.bibliogrande.com

At BiblioLife, we aim to make knowledge more accessible by making thousands of titles available to you – quickly and affordably.

Contact us:
BiblioLife
PO Box 21206
Charleston, SC 29413

CPSIA information can be obtained at www.ICGtesting.com
Printed in the USA
BVOW03s1856260913

332247BV00009B/116/A